NATIVE AMERICAN
SPIRITUALISM

NATIVE
AMERICAN
SPIRITUALISM

*An Exploration of
Indigenous Beliefs
and Cultures*

L.M. ARROYO

wellfleet
press

CONTENTS

INTRODUCTION

Despite being vibrant, dynamic, and wholly unique individual societies, Native American cultures are often painted with broad brushstrokes, and people outside of the communities themselves have little more than a basic understanding of the current realities of Native American life. Education for non-Natives is steeped in colonialism that taints the lens of truer, authentic understanding.

The only way to really understand the complexity of Native American beliefs, practices, and spirituality is by recognizing and unlearning the colonial framework that has shaped non-Native understanding of Native life and culture for centuries. This is, of course, easier said than done. It can be very difficult to go up against a lifetime of misinformation and whitewashing and open ourselves up to the hard truth about our histories, but the good news is that it isn't impossible and it can also be a joy-filled journey.

The most authentic way to do so is by connecting with the Native American community in one's own city. We all live on Indigenous land, and there is no better resource than the people who, against the odds, have persevered for centuries with their cultures intact. Knowing that this is not an option for all, those who want to learn in good faith can and should do so, seeking out resources, like this one, that make earnest attempts to parse this rich, complex history straight from legitimate, contemporary Native American sources.

The hope is that this book will serve as a resource for those looking to enrich their own understanding of Native American culture and life without adding to the harm that so many have suffered as a result of appropriation, willful ignorance, colonialism, and paternalism.

One of the biggest mistakes we can make when discussing Native American culture is to assume that it is a monolith. In fact, each Nation has a distinctly unique identity, history, and language that informs its practices and beliefs—all of which deserve careful study. In the United States alone, there are 567 federally recognized Nations, each with their own unique culture. As a result of having been misrepresented for so long, realistic, insightful, and nuanced portrayals are more important than ever before. Making blanket statements about Native Americans reinforces colonialist perspectives and is especially egregious when you take into account that in many ways the various Native American cultures in North America are actually much more distinct and diverse than what is generally considered to be "American culture."

Native American cultures and religious practices are very often quite deeply rooted in their geographical location. A southwest desert Nation may have an entirely different set of rituals, spiritual beliefs, ceremonial rites, and deities than one from the northeast. This is just one of many factors that influence the various nuances within an individual Nation's culture, but it is a helpful thing to literally try to visualize when attempting to understand how these differences have evolved over the centuries.

That said, there are commonalities between Nations, the most important among them being the astonishing reality that despite 500 years of colonization and repeated attempts at physical and cultural genocide, Native American people, their cultures, and spiritual Traditions have survived. Their resilience is indicative of the depth of their beliefs and the strength of their ties to their communities, histories, and culture. Native American Nations are currently in the midst of cultural reclamation and healing despite a lack of meaningful reparations. However, federal recognition and the important protections that go along with them have helped to give them some of the resources they need to bolster their communities. These efforts include working to reestablish the traditional names of Indigenous Nations and increased efforts to teach young Native Americans their language and history, among many other things. The importance of educating the younger members of the communities cannot be understated.

And while differences abound, there are common threads that run between different Native American Nations. This includes the fact that Native Americans do not view their spiritual practices in the same way other cultures regard the dictionary definition of "religion." It is less about "believing" their religion than it is living and breathing it, oftentimes in a literal sense with the Sacred Pipe (see page 117). It melts into every aspect of life—there is no separation between art, work, love, nature, family, and religion—they are all one. All of this informs a lifestyle that is deeply conscious of its effects on the natural world around them, and an ability to maintain high levels of respect for the environment, animals, and each other.

There are also pan-Indigenous beliefs and common themes within their spiritual traditions, including their relationship to nature, animals, and even the way they view and experience time. Unlike linear time, which constantly moves forward, many Native American Traditions are centered around cyclical time. Cyclical time moves in loops, like the seasons, which means that through The Creator, the universe is constantly giving people opportunities for renewal, restoration, comfort, and hope. Many Nations honor the passing of cyclical time with renewal Ceremonies, which are not only celebrations of a changing season, but which they believe also help to sustain life and growth.

Native American Oral Traditions also reference an era known as "Creation," which refers to the period of time when the world was created. Even though each Nation has its own Creation Oral Tradition, they all take place during Mythic Time. It was during this period that The Creator, also referred to in various Nations as "The Great Mysterious" or "Great Spirit," brought forth life. "The Creator" is the term that has become widely accepted by Native American Peoples to describe the supreme being who created the world and all of its living beings, then intentionally placed them on specific lands and gave them laws to live by. During the process of creating the world, Native Americans believe that The Creator imbued the actual geographical land, beings, and their rituals with spiritual power. It is just one of many reasons why their Native homelands are so incredibly important to them. It is not just the place they were born; it is where The Creator specifically intended them to live.

Many of the ceremonies and beliefs that Native Americans hold to this day stem from events that they believe occurred during Mythic Time. Native Americans see these events not as legends or myths akin to fairy tales; they believe and know they are part of their historical record. As such, it is diminishing and offensive for historians, anthropologists, and other non-Natives to reduce them to mere fictional cautionary tales or parables.

APPROPRIATION VS. APPRECIATION

While any culture can be appropriated, one of the most casually and commonly appropriated and flagrantly disrespected cultures is that of Native Americans. It seems to be almost socially acceptable, and most people either turn a blind eye or don't even fully have the ability to recognize it when it occurs.

Cultural appropriation comes in many forms, but these days it is very commonly seen in fashion. A good example of this is when non-Native people wear headdresses or Native American beads and jewelry at music festivals—it's become shockingly commonplace despite the fact that it's extremely problematic. It also happens in the form of co-opting language, such as flippantly using the term "Sprit Animal" with no regard to what it actually means to Native Americans and the fact that the community has repeatedly asked non-Native people in no uncertain terms to refrain from using that phrase. Even the casual use of Dream Catchers in one's home can be a form of appropriation. They are so ubiquitous that most people don't even know that they originate in Native American Culture.

In contrast, cultural appreciation is a wonderful way to enjoy and learn more about cultures different than one's own. For example, researching, seeking out, and buying authentic art, jewelry, or artisanal objects from Indigenous artisans and using them in an appropriate, respectful manner is a great form of cultural appreciation that also financially supports Indigenous communities. However, purchasing trendy "Indigenous-inspired" items that have been mass-produced by big-box retailers could be considered to be a form of cultural appropriation.

A more unexpected form of appropriation, however, is when non-Native people co-opt Native American spirituality while searching for their own spiritual paths. While this doesn't always stem from maliciousness, it is still ill-advised.

It is absolutely to be expected that so many people are searching for answers during such challenging times. It can be hard to understand why difficult things happen. A pandemic, childhood illness, accidents, climate change, unexpected deaths—these deeply traumatic experiences are incredibly destabilizing and leave people desperate for peace of mind. People experiencing loss, pain, and other types of grief or confusion may attempt to adopt Native American Traditions without really understanding them.

Even truly sincere attempts at modeling one's spiritual life after the beliefs and practices of Native Americans could potentially be seen as its own new brand of colonialism. Patching together traditions and beliefs from various Nations and even other world religions to suit an individual's needs and fill a spiritual void is inauthentic and disrespectful. It is offensive to deny the fact that Native American Ceremonies are the result of very specific worldviews and cannot and should not be mixed and matched at one's leisure. It's especially abhorrent given the history of forced assimilation that Native Americans have had to endure, and how difficult it has been to maintain their spiritual practices amidst the violence of colonization.

One-size-fits-all spirituality is not indicative of true Native American culture and beliefs. Spirituality for spirituality's sake is an exploitation of these complex, long-held, and deeply rooted beliefs, no matter how benign the intentions may be.

However, what non-Natives can do is learn about these traditions, ruminate on their deeper meanings, and look inwards to see how the truths that speak to them from these traditions can be applied to their own lives and problems in non offensive ways. This is what we aim to do here—to lay the groundwork for understanding Native American beliefs without appropriation. So instead of taking a Native American tradition or ritual and attempting to practice it yourself, look at the bigger picture. How can the Native American philosophy of never taking more from the Earth than you need in that moment inform your feelings about environmental conservation? How can you live out the Haudenosaunee Confederacy's ideals of the Seventh Generation in your daily life? How can you then take this information and put it into action in your day-to-day routine?

At every step along the way, we must interrogate our intentions and take in what we are learning without making it about ourselves. Cultural sensitivity is always appreciated, but it is of the utmost importance when discussing and learning about a group of people who have been denied their humanity and basic rights for centuries.

What you'll find within these pages is a look at eight different Native American Nations and their beliefs and practices. The hope is that these glimpses into several beautiful, varied cultures can provide a window to people who have been disregarded for far too long. Each of these Nations brings a rich and complicated set of spiritual beliefs and practices to the table, and they shed light on the broader way in which Native Americans view the world and live their lives. Exercises, creative activities, and even bits of trivia will be provided throughout to help you cement the concepts and even see how they may already be reflected in your everyday life. Through these we will strive to appreciate the beauty of Native

American Traditions, while not claiming them in a disrespectful way by rolling elements into our own practice.

The goal here is not to pick apart aspects of Native American rituals and take them for our own or to supplement a spiritual practice, but to gain a better understanding and awareness of the intricacies of Native American beliefs. It is also possible to find comfort and a greater understanding of our place in the world, expand the limits of our compassion, and be inspired by the way Native Americans view and treat the planet at large, which is largely shaped by their spiritual beliefs and practices. By broadening our foundational understanding of the topic, we can further deepen our appreciation as well.

We cannot talk about Native American spirituality, beliefs, and cultural practices without the larger overall context of the United States' history. To do so would be a disservice to Native Americans. We'll discuss it broadly in the next chapter and then specifically in regard to certain Nations as they come up.

A NOTE ON CAPITALIZATION

As you read this book, you may notice that certain terms that would not ordinarily be capitalized (think Oral Traditions, Traditional Knowledge, Sacred Stories, and more) *are* capitalized in an Indigenous context. This is because they are Traditional Indigenous terms that hold deep, sacred meanings for Native American people. This simple style choice is preferred by the community and helps to avoid repeating or contributing to past harm.

CHAPTER 1

DEFINING ORAL TRADITIONS AND TRADITIONAL KNOWLEDGE

B efore jumping into the more complicated intricacies that make
up the beliefs and spiritual practices of various Native American
Nations, it's important to provide context for how these beliefs have
been recorded and passed down through generations since time
immemorial. There is no Rosetta Stone for Native American languages
or history, which means that any current-day information we have
regarding Native American life has been passed down through word
of mouth. This "collecting and passing on" system of information
throughout the generations is what is now referred to as Oral
Traditions and Traditional Knowledge.

ORAL TRADITIONS
VS. TRADITIONAL KNOWLEDGE

What many non-Natives grew up referring to as myths are actually called Oral Traditions. This covers a range of spiritual topics, including everything from Creation Stories to religious rites, rituals, and more. Traditional Knowledge encompasses more practical everyday information, such as how to build homes, make medicine, and tend to the natural world. Native Americans have always held their histories, beliefs, and culture close, and this is in large part why their spiritual and physical lives are so interconnected. This method of imparting information also serves to cultivate respect throughout the generations, both for young people who revere their Elders and the knowledge they keep, and the older folks who realize that they are merely custodians of the Earth for the younger generations to come. By keeping these practices alive to these days, Native American people remain connected to themselves, their cultures, and their community at large.

Prior to colonization, when Native Americans were forced to learn how to read and write English, they did not have a written language. But that doesn't mean that their language, art, or forms of communication were in any way inferior. In fact, the opposite is true. The wealth of information that each Indigenous Nation carries and has passed down orally throughout the centuries was also supplemented with other methods of documentation and communication. They were often more concrete and made of physical materials, and include dramatic interpretations, dance performances, petroglyphs, scrolls, Totems, Wampum Belts, masks, and more. These different mediums can be used as a way of reinforcing storytelling.

This, alongside repetition, can help the listener memorize these Oral Traditions so that they can one day pass them on as well.

The fact that Native Americans were historically non literate was and still is used as a way to belittle their intelligence, vast amounts of knowledge, and personal value. But the fact remains that Oral Tradition enriches and brings to life Native American stories in a way that the written word simply cannot. This extends to nearly every aspect of life—from the names they call each other, to the phrases and descriptors they use while speaking, to the nuanced, subtle ways that they communicate, which non-Natives with untrained ears cannot connect with or understand.

Art is one of the many ways through which we can more deeply convey our emotions, thoughts, and experiences aside from written language. What art or activity do you use to convey how you feel when you experience complicated emotions and words just aren't adequate?

CREATION

As was touched on earlier, much of what shapes Native American beliefs has to do with their faith in the events that occurred during Creation. While each Nation's Creation story differs, all embrace the belief in the era during which The Creator formed the Earth, cosmos, oceans, animals, plants, and people. It was during this time that The Creator imbued the land with power—power through which The Creator gave the Spirits and humans their important Ceremonies, rites, and rituals, and with which people learned to live in harmony with the natural world. It is through Oral Tradition that the information regarding the events that occurred during Creation, along with the Ceremonies and practices that were bestowed to them by The Creator, have been passed down through the generations.

ORAL TRADITIONS

Unlike what you may have heard referred to as "folklore" or "legends," Oral Traditions are stories that are spiritually connected to the land, ancestors, and the particular Nation from which they come. Oral Traditions are stories that have been told for centuries, if not millennia, and many of these Oral Traditions are Sacred Stories—essentially, each Nation's origin story. While the term *folklore* is commonly used in anthropology and art history, it is an archaic and offensive term when applied to Indigenous Peoples' cultural practices because it implies that they are inferior and illegitimate in comparison to those of Western cultures.

TRADITIONAL KNOWLEDGE

Like Oral Traditions and Sacred Stories, practical information was and still is passed down orally in order to ensure each Nation's continued survival and prosperity. This wider category of information is called Traditional Knowledge. It serves as a comprehensive education that was, and still remains, vital to Native American communities. The range of topics can include anything from the scientific—such as medicines, biology, climate patterns, and animal migrations—to practical living concerns like architecture and how to use fire for forest management. On the whole, Traditional Knowledge is not considered Sacred, though some of it is. Predominantly, it is applicative information. That said, one can't flippantly write or discuss any element of Traditional Knowledge as they see fit, because in some cases it just isn't appropriate to do so. This applies to both Native and non-Native people alike.

INDIGENOUS PROTOCOLS

For non-Natives, it's important to understand that both Traditional Knowledge and Oral Traditions are Indigenous cultural property, which means that Indigenous Protocols must be followed when discussing and sharing certain sensitive Traditional Knowledge and Oral Traditions.

Indigenous Protocols for Traditional Knowledge and Oral Traditions refer to Native American guidelines that dictate that not everything is appropriate for wider knowledge outside of their communities. Oftentimes, Traditional Knowledge holds information about various topics that have a Sacred significance, while Oral Traditions have Sacred Stories. What might seem like a mundane story to a non-Native might be steeped in spiritual meaning for a Native American person. But it's not just non-Natives who have to observe Native American Protocols; certain Protocols apply to Native Americans as well.

There are also some stories that can only be told by certain families or Clans, or only by women or men, or only during certain seasons. For example, some Nations consider it bad luck to share Oral Traditions about the Thundergods until the stormy season has passed. There are also many Oral Traditions that can only be told during the winter season, which is generally considered the time when communities sit around a fire for warmth and share with each other. Some Oral Traditions can only be spoken during specific Ceremonies in order to invoke the Spirits or The Creator, and to do otherwise would strip it of meaning and make it impossible for Spirits to be present.

Understandably, Native Americans take offense when anyone breaches these Protocols, but especially when it comes to non-Natives, because doing so is essentially an extension of colonial attitudes and oppression. That doesn't even begin to take into account that the threat of these attitudes distorts the lens through which the purpose and meaning of the stories are meant to be understood. These are important things to take into consideration when reading, learning about, and studying Native American Traditions as non-Native people. Being thoughtful and aware of what is appropriate at all times is the most respectful way to move forward on this journey to better understanding and appreciating Native American culture. You can listen without participating. You can ask questions so that you receive understanding rather than taking it on your own terms. Choosing to read this book demonstrates an inherent curiosity that is appreciated and welcomed.

Above all, it is important to remember that because Native American Oral Traditions and Traditional Knowledge are legally Indigenous intellectual property, authorship of this information belongs only to the specific Nations that are the source of this information. So to impart this knowledge without permission or the guidance of the Indigenous Community only serves to cause more damage, no matter how unintentional or even well-intentioned it may be. If any course of action seems unclear, it's best to always simply ask.

As discussed earlier, Native American people are in the process of reclaiming their cultures, and that includes, in many cases, changing their Tribal names back from the ones that were given to them during the colonial era. Moving forward, you'll notice that this text will make an effort to place Native Americans firmly in the present, both geographically and culturally. For example, members of what many of us have known as the Iroquois Confederacy are now commonly referred to as the Haudenosaunee. Unlearning colonial points of view is key to understanding what is at the heart of Native American culture, and calling them by their true names is as good a place as ever to start. That said, we'll touch on instances where there are discrepancies, even within individual Nations, about what people would like to call themselves—and it can vary based on region or even just personal preference.

Expanding one's knowledge about Native American cultures, beliefs, and spiritual practices can enrich non-Natives' perspectives in many ways. The more education we have on cultures, philosophies, and outlooks that are different from our own, the more we are able to respect and understand individuals with different backgrounds. The hope is that by gaining a richer and deeper understanding of the more nuanced aspects of Native American spirituality, non-Natives can broaden their own frame of reference. Let these beliefs challenge your own perspectives and find out how they might help you see the world in a way you wouldn't have otherwise. For example, how does gaining a deeper understanding of the Chinook's Potlatch Ceremony change or challenge your own perceptions of what it means to enact generosity within your own community? How can you put into practice the Seventh Generation value in your own life? How can you take what you learn about Native American people's appreciation and devotion to the land and apply it to the environment in which you live? By ruminating on the larger meaning of these values and practices, non-Natives can look for ways to find more meaning, joy, and peace in their lives, without co-opting, copying, or appropriating them.

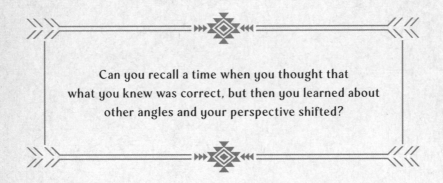

Can you recall a time when you thought that what you knew was correct, but then you learned about other angles and your perspective shifted?

The relationship between Native Americans and the United States government remains fraught. Centuries of attempted genocide, violence, and forced assimilation have had a profound impact on Native American people and their various practices. Depending on where they lived, they may have been forced to leave their ancestral lands, were obligated to convert to Christianity, had some of their most important Ceremonies banned, or were murdered by the thousands. To this day, there have been no meaningful reparations on behalf of the United States government, and it was only in 2022 that the Canadian government agreed to a mass financial settlement with their First Nations.

The ramifications of this entwined history are deep and complicated. As you'll see as we move forward, no Native American Nation has been spared the long-lasting damage that is done when people are uprooted and denied their basic humanity. All of this informs the way that they approach their spiritual life, cultural practices, and relationships with each other. Despite all that they have been through, there is no better word to describe their commitment to the advancement of their cultures than *devotion*.

Many people believe that the United States government should pay financial reparations to Native Americans as a way to make amends for the centuries of disease outbreaks, land theft, and genocide. This has not yet happened, but there are a few reasons why a Native American person or group might have received compensation. Certain specific federal laws compensated Native People for stolen land, like the 1971 Alaskan Native Claims Settlement Act, which settled all land claims against the government by Alaskan Natives.

MARKING
THE PASSAGE OF TIME

All of us mark the passing of time, whether in a larger cultural context, within our family units, or individually. For example, in Judaism, one way the passage of time is marked is through acknowledging the past. Yom Kippur is a day of atonement for past transgressions and an opportunity to move forward in time.

Considering what you've learned thus far regarding the passage of time and the ways that it is marked in various Native American cultures, think on the following questions.

1. Reflect on the ways in which you mark the passage of time in your life.

2. What ceremonies and rituals do you perform?

3. Are you surprised to find that there are more than you previously believed?

4. Reach out to members of your community of different generations and ask them about the significant moments in their lives.

5. Do they differ from your own?

CHAPTER 2

THE SEVEN WISE MEN OF THE LENAPE NATION

The Lenni-Lenape, most commonly known as the Lenape, are a wonderful starting point for anyone on a journey to learn more about Native American culture because they are the common ancestral root for many other Native American Nations. The Lenape Nation is made up of multiple different communities that share Lenape culture, with at least three different dialects of the language, including Munsee, Unalachtigo, and Unami. The Lenape People's homeland includes southeastern New York, northern Delaware, eastern Pennsylvania, and New Jersey, as well as five federally recognized Nations in Oklahoma, Wisconsin, and Ontario. Manhattan (or Manahatta to the Lenape) was its center, but centuries of colonialism and genocide forced the displacement of the Lenape throughout the United States and Canada.

Neighbors to the Iroquois, Shawnee, and Susquehannock, the Lenape Tribal Nation has also included the Nanticoke People of the Delmarva between the Chesapeake and Delaware Bays since about the 1600s. They are all collectively known as the Nanticoke Lenni-Lenape Tribal Nation.

The Lenape have been caretakers of these lands for over 10,000 years and were actually the first Nation to have federally protected land set aside for them in New Jersey. They were the first Indian Nation to sign a treaty with the United States, which allowed American troops to pass through their territory and gave the Lenape the ability to sell goods like food, horses, and other supplies to the United States. To this day, the Lenape have Tribal grounds, called Cohanzick, in Fairfield Township, New Jersey. They have lived here for hundreds of years and it's where one can find their Tribal community center and Ceremonial ground.

CEREMONIES

There are many aspects of the culture that can help one gain insight into the Lenape's many closely held spiritual beliefs, and a good way to do so is by investigating and understanding the Nation's Creation story and some of their most important Ceremonies. The Lenape Creation story is the origin not only of their spiritual beliefs but of many of their utilitarian daily practices as well. It serves as a guide for everything—from how to keep the peace when there is discord to how to build a Sacred Fire, construct a home, and be good stewards of the land with which they have been entrusted.

SEASONAL CEREMONIES

Like most Native American Nations, the Lenape centered many of their religious ceremonies around the seasons, such as the Midwinter Solstice, Pooxit (the Time of the Falling Leaves), Mecoammawi Gischuch (the Time When the Shad Fish Return), and Winaminge (the Time of the Roasting Ears of Corn). Because they see time as cyclical as opposed to linear, it is marked from spring to spring, and the length of the months vary depending on the climate and environment. The flowers of spring herald the return of the Shad fish to local waters, while berries mark the summer season.

However, not all Ceremonies are centered around nature or the changing seasons. This includes the Naming Ceremony, when all Lenape People are gifted their true names by members of their community, and the Big House Ceremony, a twelve-day celebration of Thanksgiving. Both of these Ceremonies, which we'll go into greater detail on later, give key insights into the Lenape People's values and belief systems, including how they view their relationship to each other and the land.

The Naming Ceremony is a good example of how deeply each individual's identity is interwoven with their community, nature, and unique personal experiences. Along with other ceremonies, including the Big House Ceremony, it reinforces the sense of community and duty to The Creator. The Big House Ceremony, like any Thanksgiving celebration, gives great insight into the things that sustain the Lenape, both spiritually and physically.

As you read, try to find commonalities not just between the Lenape and other Native American Nations, but with yourself as well. What resonates with you? What aspects of their cultural viewpoint bring to mind the significance of your own community, name, and the things for which you are grateful? Do you see any common threads between the Lenape's beliefs and Judeo-Christian beliefs?

THE CREATION STORY

The Lenape believe that before Creation there was nothing but a dark empty space, and the spirit of The Creator fell asleep and dreamt of a world filled with nature and all those who inhabit it, including animals and people. When The Creator awoke, He first created "helper Spirits" to help him begin to manifest this world. He called on the Grandfather of the North, the Grandfather of the West, the Grandfather of the East, and the Grandmother of the South to channel their dreams and thoughts into creating the sun, moon, stars, heavens, and Earth, until everything The Creator had dreamed of had come to fruition. One of the last things they did was create a special shimmering tree, from whose root the First Man sprung. The tree then bent down and kissed the ground, and from that spot arose First Woman.

Everyone lived in harmony, working together on jobs given to them by The Creator. Deer were sent to eat underbrush to clear space for trees to grow. Squirrels were tasked with collecting nuts and burying them so vegetation would flourish, and the Lenape People were made to be caretakers of the land. All was well until humans began to fight over the tooth of a bear that could give the owners magical powers. The resulting wars caused so much strife that people moved away and made new Tribes and languages.

When The Creator saw what was happening, he sent a spirit named Nanapush to help reunite the people. Nanapush went to the top of one of the mountains and made what was to become the first Sacred Fire, which sent up smoke that drew people from far and wide to investigate its source. Once everyone had arrived, Nanapush gave them a pipe created from a sumac branch and soapstone and told them to use it to smoke a Sacred plant, tobacco, which had been given to him by The Creator.

He called on them to smoke a pipe together whenever there were important Councils, Ceremonies, and even disagreements. The belief is that the smoke will go into every person, then when it is blown out, everyone's thoughts and prayers would blend, making it possible to reach decisions that are right for everyone and everything.

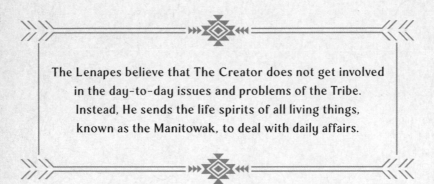

The Lenapes believe that The Creator does not get involved in the day-to-day issues and problems of the Tribe. Instead, He sends the life spirits of all living things, known as the Manitowak, to deal with daily affairs.

The tobacco plant, one of the four Sacred Herbs.

THE LENAPE, THE COSMOS, AND THE NATURAL WORLD

Like so many Nations, the Lenape's spiritual connection with the natural world is deeply entrenched in their literal, physical closeness to, and dependence on, natural resources. As such, their only recourse is to fully surrender to nature as the supreme wellspring of power. This vulnerability is the source of their belief that all natural elements are interwoven—from the plants to the sea, animals, and cosmos.

In fact, a popular Lenape Oral Tradition called the Seven Wise Men perfectly captures the circular dynamic that the Lenape have between themselves, their spirituality, and the celestial world.

THE SEVEN WISE MEN

This Oral Tradition tells of a time when seven wise men lived among the Lenape People. Both day and night, people would come to them constantly, seeking their advice. There was no rest for the weary. It became so overwhelming and exhausting that they decided they needed to get away to find some peace and quiet. They went up into the mountains and turned themselves into giant boulders. One day, a young man who was out hunting came upon the boulders and noticed that there was something a little off about them; they were different than any boulders he'd ever encountered before. He was so moved by them that he started coming back every day. After some time, he realized that if he spoke to them, the rocks would respond in kind. He was shocked and a little scared, but couldn't bring himself to stop going to see them.

Before long, he went back to the village and told the people about finding seven magical, wise stones that answered all his pressing life questions. People started leaving the village and going up the mountain to ask the boulders questions of their own. Eventually, the seven wise men came to the conclusion that they would have to change and find a way once more to attain that peace and quiet they desperately craved. So they went to the very top of the mountain and turned themselves into beautiful and grand cedar trees. They could feel the cool breeze blowing through their needles and finally felt the bliss of total serenity. Understandably, it wasn't long before people started noticing that these seven beguiling and graceful trees were singing beautiful songs. The people quickly realized that these were the seven wise men and started going to them for guidance and answers. Once again, the seven wise men asked themselves what they should do to find stillness and silence. They looked up into the heavens and decided to turn into seven stars, so they would be able to look down on the people who wouldn't be able to come up and bother them. So they turned themselves into the seven stars that became known as the Pleiades, where they remain today.

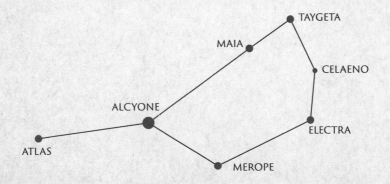

The Pleiades Star Cluster

THE STORY OF THE MAPLE TREE

The fluid boundaries between the Lenape, their spirituality, and the natural world only serve to reinforce their beliefs that they must remain deferential and in harmony with nature, even though they have the ability to cultivate and manage resources.

The Story of the Maple Tree also serves to support these beliefs. It tells the Oral Tradition of how the Lenape first learned to tap maple trees for their syrup, a vital resource for the community that is treated with care and reverence. It states that a long time ago, the maple tree was one of the most beautiful and loved trees in all of the natural world. But one day, a large collection of bugs crawled into the maple's bark, making the tree itchy and driving him crazy. Despite the maple tree's many branches, he could not bend down to reach all his itchy parts, so he called out to his friends in the animal kingdom to ask for relief. A beaver, a little mouse, and a bear all offered to help, but each ultimately came to the conclusion that any assistance would likely lead to the maple tree's untimely demise. Finally, a small bird flew by and told the tree that he would ask his woodpecker friends for help.

The woodpeckers flew over and started pecking at the tree, eventually getting all the bugs out of him. The tree was very happy, and everyone went on with their lives. A few years later there was a drought. The creeks and rivers dried up and all the animals were very thirsty. The maple tree heard them lamenting their situation and remembered how the animals had helped him in his time of need. He

called out to the bird and asked him to tell the woodpeckers to come back. He told them to peck deep into his bark until sap began to run out of him, and that way everyone could drink the sap and quench their thirst. This gift saved everyone until the rains returned and they were able to drink water again. It was through this gift from the maple tree to the animals that the Lenape learned how to tap maple trees and make maple syrup. Maple syrup was treasured year-round but became a precious commodity to them every winter when there were no berries to pick and sweet things to enjoy, making the maple tree's gift all the more precious.

THE BIG HOUSE CEREMONY

The Big House refers to the central religious building and is used exclusively for an annual Ceremony in the fall to thank The Creator for the last year's blessings (such as a plentiful harvest or good hunting) and pray for protection and good fortune in the year to come. It could be considered their Thanksgiving celebration, and usually takes place in October. It is also known as the Gamwing or Xingwikaon.

The Big House itself holds many clues as to the Lenape's most precious beliefs. The structure of the building is a symbolic representation of the world and has a central column that connects the sky to the Earth, surrounded by walls facing the four cardinal directions.

The architectural concept of the Big House is based on a specific section of their Creation Oral Tradition, when The Creator spoke to the Lenape in their dreams and told them that war and discord were the result of neglecting their spiritual relationship. The Lenape were directed to build a house that recreated the cosmos and instructed on how to hold a Ceremony that was imbued with the power to sustain the Nation through time. The house is a symbol of the universe, with details for interior decoration laid out by The Creator. As a result, the Lenape were responsible for converting a divine idea into something physical that is tangible, palpable, and functional—the form of a house.

They had to choose between their circular wigwam or the rectangular shape of their longhouses, and ultimately chose the longhouse design. Not only is it better equipped to support communal gatherings and functions, but it is also easier to orient with the four cardinal points. The eastern door faces the direction of the rising sun and moon and represents the beginning of time. The western door faces the setting of the sun and moon and symbolizes both the end of everything and the Good White Path, which is the road one travels from birth until death. There are two smoke holes in the roof, one above each of the Sacred Fires, which traditionally only men could light.

The Lenape believe that the act of holding a twelve-day Big House Ceremony helps preserve the balance of the world, continuing the cycle of time. During the ceremony, preselected individuals share their dreams and visions, sing songs, and dance around the fire as a form of worship. Red cedar, considered sacred, is burned to purify all people and things, and a Spiritual Leader calls on The Creator to bring health, peace, and prosperity to the people. When the fires are extinguished on the twelfth day, the ceremony is finished, and the Big House is closed for another year.

Do you have a community gathering place? Like the
Big House, most of us have places where we find solace,
gather with our loved ones, and celebrate special moments.
This can be a matriarch's home, a community center,
a religious building, or even a park or weekly gathering.
Where do you go to find your community? Is it different
than the community gathering places you visited as a child?

THE NAMING CEREMONY

One of the most significant and sacred religious Ceremonies in Lenape culture is their Naming Ceremony. Traditionally, Lenape babies are not named at birth; they are gifted their names once they are older. The chosen names are always meaningful and are representative of qualities that are specific to that person. The name can be chosen to reflect certain defining characteristics or strengths in the individual, personified by an animal that symbolizes those traits. The name can honor significant events or people from that person's life or be representative of natural elements (such as flowers, trees, the sky) that are significant to this person, their values, and their personality.

A Lenape person's Naming Ceremony can be held at any point during their lives. Some receive more than one name during their lifetime to reflect significant changes that may have occurred, and there are also instances of people not having a given name until close to their deaths.

Often, the person who is being gifted a name must first request permission from an Elder. Once the Elder has granted permission, preparations for the ceremony can begin while the Elder considers the appropriate name. It can come to them in a vision, in a dream, or in an unexpected moment of reflection. They keep it a secret until it's time for the ceremony.

When it is time to perform the Naming Ceremony, the individual's family, friends, and members of the Tribal Community gather in the Sacred Circle. The circle is an invocation of cyclical time and represents the continuity of the seasons, the circle of life, and wholeness. At the start of the ceremony, each person is smudged, or cleansed, with the sacred smoke of lavender, sweetgrass, and sage.

After that, the Seven Directions and Spirit Keepers are invited to join for protection and guidance. The Seven Directions include North, South, East, West, Father Sky, Mother Earth, and the Great Spirit. Then the individual is blessed and anointed with the four elements: air, earth, water, and fire. The community prays together as the Elder or otherwise gifting member of the community shares the gifted name with the Spiritual Leader, explaining why it was specifically chosen for this person. The newly named member is then escorted around the circle as their name is announced, and they are introduced to The Creator. This joyful celebration is then sealed with music and dance.

INVESTIGATING
YOUR OWN NAME

While not all cultures have naming ceremonies, many families have rituals or traditions that accompany the arrival and naming of a new child, such as a christening or 100 Days celebration, which is an important Korean event that takes place after a child is born.

The process of selecting a name for a loved one varies from person to person. Some pass down family names, others wait to see what a new baby looks like before deciding definitively, and others spend months scouring baby name books for the one that looks just right. However you arrive at it, there's no denying that your name has significant influence on how you see yourself and how others perceive you as well.

After ruminating on the questions below, create a keepsake collage in celebration of your own name and what it means to you.

>> What emotions, images, and memories does your name call to mind?

>> How has your given name uniquely shaped your personal identity throughout the course of your life?

>> Would you have picked differently for yourself if you could? Have you?

>> What significance does this new name hold for you? How has or how would a new name change the way you view yourself?

CHAPTER 3

MIDWINTER WITH THE HAUDENOSAUNEE NATION

If you grew up in North America, there's a good chance you learned about the Iroquois—just without the added context that they're actually an alliance of Native Nations who have always called themselves the Haudenosaunee Confederacy. It was the French who called them the Iroquois, while the English knew them as the League of Five Nations. Initially, five Nations were brought together to form a Confederacy—the Mohawk, Oneida, Onondaga, Cayuga, and Seneca Nations. It wasn't until the early 1600s that the Tuscarora peacefully joined the Confederacy after migrating from the south. All six were united under Haudenosaunee Traditional Law, with complementary values, beliefs, and Traditions that inform their common cultures.

The Haudenosaunee believe it was the prophet peacemaker Hiawatha who founded the Confederacy during Mythic Time, making them the first participatory democracy of all time. Some believe the Confederacy's constitution was a model for the American constitution, though it differs from the latter because it blends both laws and values. They were united by a common goal: to live in harmony with each other and facilitate a peaceful means of decision-making. Each Nation has its own Council to handle internal issues, but a Grand Council oversees the affairs of all the Nations in the Confederacy.

Traditionally and presently, the majority of the Haudenosaunee People reside in what is now known as New York, though they also live in various other states and parts of Canada. The Mohawk People, traditionally called the Kanien'kehaka, are spread throughout eight different communities in Quebec, Ontario, and New York. The Seneca, or Onondowahgah, are located in western New York, Oklahoma, and Ontario. They are also the only Nation to own a United States city: Salamanca, New York. The Oneida Nation (Onyota'ake) reside in New York, Canada, and Wisconsin. The Cayuga People, or Guyohkohnyoh, are named after their Traditional Territory surrounding the Finger Lakes in New York. They reside in New York, Oklahoma, and Ontario. The Onondaga (Ononda'gega') Nation reside just south of Syracuse, New York.

The Nations of the Haudenosaunee Confederacy

The Mohawk — The People of the Flint
Oneida — The People of the Upright Stone
Onondaga — The People of the Hills
Cayuga — The People of the Great Swamp
Seneca — The People of the Great Hill
Tuscarora — The People of the Shirt

Haudenosaunee means People of the Longhouse, and their tradition of communal living emphasized their treasured sense of togetherness. Traditional values like sharing daily labor, being respectful and loyal to their family and Clan, and being thankful to nature and The Creator for the sustenance they provided were paramount. But another core value within the Haudenosaunee community is the Seventh Generation. The Seventh Generation value takes into consideration the descendants who will inherit the Earth. Chiefs reflect on the impact that their decisions will have on those who have not yet been born, and everyone is encouraged to live their lives as if they are borrowing the world from future generations. The Seventh Generation value also helps to emphasize the importance of keeping their cultural practices, languages, and ceremonies alive. It's vital that future generations are able to participate in and practice Haudenosaunee culture.

These values are expressed in their daily routine as well as in celebrations and ceremonies like the Midwinter Ceremony and the Sun Dance. And it's also the reason why these Ceremonies are still practiced to this very day. Both the Midwinter Ceremony and the Sun Dance are acts of thanksgiving that acknowledge the gifts that they have received as well as the ones that are on the way. They also believe that performing these Ceremonies are paramount to maintaining the cycle of life, and that these, and the many others that are performed throughout the year, keep cyclical time moving in perpetuity.

THE LONGHOUSE

The Haudenosaunee's traditional home is integral to their cultural and individual identities. The longhouse was the hub of all activity where generations came together to live among each other and foster familial relations. These rectangular structures were up to 200 feet (61 m) long and 18 feet (5.5 m) wide, accommodating as many as 100 people at times, though it was probably often more like thirty people on average. Cord was made from wood fibers and used to bring thick slabs of bark that had been stripped from elm trees that were used as shingles for the walls and roof, while the doors at either end of the house were made from bark or animal hide.

These houses were made to be shared with entire extended Clan families that had a common female ancestor. They housed parents and children, plus grandparents, aunts, uncles, and cousins. They worked together in all aspects of keeping and running the house. When young Haudenosaunee married, the husband would leave his Clan and go live in his wife's longhouse, though they'd maintain close relationships with their own Clans as well.

The Haudenosaunee trace their bloodlines through women, who are the leaders within their Clans. Women are honored members of their communities. The Clan Mothers select the male representatives to the Tribal Council, the Chiefs, and have veto power over the men's decisions. They also manage all of the longhouse's internal affairs and oversee all aspects of agriculture, from farming to equitable food distribution. It is women who are responsible for planting, cultivating, and harvesting.

Wood screens were used as walls to create cozy individual rooms that housed smaller immediate family units. These rooms were all equipped with a low, narrow platform that did double duty as a bed at night and a seating area during the day. They were covered with reed or corn-husk mats and animal hides to provide comfort and warmth, and one could tuck away special, personally significant items in little dugouts underneath the sleeping platform, such as jewelry, Sacred items, and more. About 5 to 7 feet (1.5 to 2 m) above the low platform there was usually another similarly sized one, almost like a bunk bed, for additional storage. The rooms also had a storage closet along areas of the walls that didn't have seating benches, where people could keep other personal items.

These individual apartments had a small doorway that opened up into a corridor that ran the entire length of the longhouse, and families shared common fire pits in the space across from them. These fire pits were used for cooking, heating, and as a light source at night.

The longhouses were actually windowless, with dome-like curved roofs and smoke holes set apart in roughly 20-foot (6 m) intervals that provided both ventilation and light. Bark and hide were used to seal them during inclement weather.

Nowadays, the Haudenosaunee live in homes made of modern materials, just like Western Europeans no longer live in log cabins. But the spirit of the communal life in a longhouse remains a focal point of the culture at large. The emphasis on mutual support while conducting daily tasks such as child minding, cooking, hunting, and more while living in the longhouse now directly correlates to the way the Haudenosaunee value their communities' contributions and lean on each other for support.

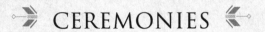

CEREMONIES

The Haudenosaunee have many Ceremonies throughout the year, usually in accordance with the cycles of the moon and seasonal changes. They are a way for the Haudenosaunee to give thanks to The Creator, the Spirits, and the natural world for health and their well-being, as well as to ask for protection from potential future challenges.

Haudenosaunee Ceremonies include:

» **MIDWINTER**—a time for renewing responsibilities for the new year.

» **MAPLE TREE**—the Haudenosaunee call on The Creator to keep those harvesting sap in the woods safe from harm.

» **THUNDER DANCE**—celebrates the return of the Thunderers, who bring rain and protect people from ferocious animals.

» **SUN DANCE**—a springtime ceremony of thanks to The Creator for peace, safety, and warmth from the Sun.

» **MOON DANCE**—women lead this ceremony, honoring the many responsibilities of the moon, including controlling the tides, plant life growing cycles, and more.

» **SEED DANCE**—this is a ceremony that honors all plant life and takes place before planting season begins.

» **STRAWBERRY**—a celebration of thanksgiving for the wild strawberry and other berries.

» **STRING BEAN**—a variety of bean dishes and soups are brought to a feast honoring the many types of beans that are part of the Haudenosaunees' diet.

» **CORN**—celebrates the life-sustaining spirit of corn.

» **HARVEST**—a feast of thanksgiving that lasts three days.

Although there are many ceremonies, we'll explore in depth the two that are vital to the proper movement of time—the Midwinter Ceremony and the Sun Dance.

THE MIDWINTER CEREMONY

The first Ceremony of the new lunar year is the Midwinter Ceremony, a celebration that lasts twenty-one days during which the Haudenosaunee give thanks to The Creator for their blessings and celebrate the joys in their lives. It's considered a time of great harmony and unity both within the community and spiritually, providing a strong sense of connection with The Creator.

Originally ordained by The Creator, the Midwinter Ceremony consists of celebratory dances, rituals, and feasts. It is the most sacred Ceremony of the Haudenosaunee ritual calendar. Depending on the appearance of the moon, it generally takes place at the end of January or beginning of February. It's a time to give thanks to The Creator and all benevolent Spirits for the good things in their lives, from their health and happiness to a good harvest, peace, and light. Each Nation in the Haudenosaunee Confederacy has slightly differing Midwinter Ceremony rituals from each other, but there are a few common through lines among the six.

The community gathers to confess sins before the start of the Midwinter rites, then on the first day three Great Feather Dances are performed. The first is to honor the members of the community who hold titles: the Chiefs and the Faith Keepers. The second is in honor of all the people in the community, from the tiniest newborn baby to the Elders. The last dance is in honor of The Creator.

Mother Earth is honored with the gathering of the ashes from wood stoves; wooden paddles are used to turn the ashes over and help to replenish Mother Earth and facilitate Her renewal.

The Tobacco Burning Thanksgiving Ceremony occurs on the third day and is burned as an acknowledgment of thanks and encouragement to all of Creation for the continuation of the cycle of life. After this, men sing songs to uplift each other's names for recognition from The Creator. Then everyone joins in during the Water Drum dance, where drums are played and people dance in an ever-moving circle that symbolizes the ongoing cycle of life.

The Peach Stone Game is played during Midwinter festivities. It's a popular gambling game that can teach lessons about life, love, and sacrifice under the guise of casual fun. It symbolizes luck bestowed on humans by The Creator and the Earth's renewal, specifically in regards to the enduring strength of fruits and vegetables that have to work so hard to survive winter. It was believed the outcome could be used to predict the success of the following year's harvest. It is also played during the Harvest and Strawberry Ceremonies.

Communal Sharing

Communal dream sharing is also an important part of the Midwinter Ceremony. The Haudenosaunee believe that dreams are not just random brain flashes or even memories, but that they give actual meaningful insight on subjects like how to cure diseases, mental health maladies, and other emotional issues. The very act of dream sharing is also considered to help rid individuals of troubling intrusive thoughts, or even help make their goals and wishes come true.

By sharing their dreams with the community, the Haudenosaunee believe that they'll be better able to find the answers to whatever concerns or issues they might have that gave rise to these specific dreams.

The members of the community who participate in this Sacred Activity do their best to offer theories, interpretations, and suggestions to help the dreamer identify what their dreams are actually telling them that they need or want. The person who is deemed to have the most accurate interpretation then has to make sure the dreamer's wish is fulfilled. This can be done by either giving them symbolic gifts or actually helping the dreamer satisfy their goal. A group of people from the Clan, sometimes called the False Face Society, can perform the necessary curing rites once the dreams have been interpreted by the Elders and the group at large.

The power to scare off evil spirits that cause illness resides primarily in the masks worn by members of the False Face Society. They are carved out of the wood of a living tree and have deep-set slits for eyes, large noses, and foreheads with spiny ridges or creases.

The Great Feather Dance

The Great Feather Dance is held on the second to last day of the Midwinter Ceremony. It gets its name from the feather headdresses worn by the dancers. Traditionally, it was a buckskin cap with a revolving eagle feather set in a spindle encircled by many other feathers. According to eighteenth-century Seneca prophet Handsome Lake, it is one of the Four Sacred Ceremonies that he proclaimed were crucial for redemption. It is a pledge to live life according to the values of longhouse living. The dancers are accompanied by two singers who sit facing each other and use turtle-shell rattles to keep rhythm.

THE SUN DANCE

The Haudenosaunee honor the relationship they and the Earth have with the sun through the Sun Dance, when they encourage the continuation of the sun's goodwill. The sun is considered to be a role model for men, who are upheld as protectors of women, children, and the elderly. The Ceremony is performed in the late spring, usually during May, when the full moon is closest to the summer solstice and the sage plant is tall and flourishing.

In keeping with Native Protocols, it is not appropriate to disclose certain specific elements of this Ceremony—those are kept private for members of the community. We do, however, have a fair bit of public information about the Haudenosaunee's traditional and present-day Sun Dances.

The start of the Ceremony is marked by three showers of arrows (or ammunition from guns) that are sent skyward to notify the sun that the Haudenosaunee intend to address him. There are war cries, then a ceremonial fire is built while the songs of thanksgiving are chanted in the hopes that the rising smoke will lift the words of those speaking and singing to the sun. The ceremonial leader of the Onondaga Nation in Ontario carries an effigy of the sun, a wooden disk painted red and yellow, and adorned with bird feathers, though not all Nations and Clans do this.

A sun pole is painted in advance and then erected, which the dancers encircle to pay homage to the sun. The ceremony was, and still is, not an easy one for the dancers. It is a grueling physical and spiritual test that they perform as a sacrifice to the rest of their Clan. They fast for days—not eating or drinking—and remain outdoors regardless of the weather. It is a relentless ordeal. On the morning of the first day they participate in a sweat bath, then paint their bodies in symbolic colors, usually red, blue, yellow, white, or black. They wear deerskin aprons, rabbit fur bracelets and anklets, and feathers in their hair.

The entire community comes together to prepare for the Sun Dance Ceremony. They organize and plan all year long, and while only one leader or small group of leaders is in charge of the Ceremony itself, many Elders give advice and input and large groups carry out the various tasks that are necessary to prepare for it.

Despite the fact that Sun Dances were one of the many Ceremonies that were prohibited as a result of colonialism, it is still performed to this day and is a symbol of the perseverance of Native Americans. These Sacred Ceremonies were held quietly and in secret during the long period of persecution that only ended very recently. Like many Ceremonies that were banned in the United States and Canada, the Sun Dance has evolved as the Haudenosaunee People have had to adapt in an effort to survive the forces of colonization. These explicit attempts on behalf of colonial governments to try to destroy Native American identity and practices has proven futile, though at a great cost. As a result, these Ceremonial dances now have dual purposes. Aside from being Traditional spiritual practices that bring them closer to and help them honor The Creator, these dances help preserve the culture and keep it alive for future generations. They are as much a teaching tool as they are a celebratory religious event. The fact that once-banned practices like the Haudenosaunee's Sun Dance have prevailed despite hundreds of years of suppression is a testament to their faith, hope, and dedication.

HOW TO PLAY
THE PEACH STONE GAME

Supplies:

> » 101 dried white beans
>
> » 1 white handkerchief per person/team
>
> » 6 peach pits, each with one side painted black
>
> » A flat-bottomed bowl

The object of the game is to shake the bowl so that all six peach pits display either their painted or unpainted side. The white beans are used in the same way that you'd use poker chips in a casino—for betting. Everyone must gamble something of value for the proverbial pot, as long as it isn't red or shiny. There is not a lot of accessible information on why these particular instructions were given, so when in doubt it's best to just keep with tradition.

Players start with six beans each, which means six chances to shake the peach stones and hope they land in a uniform manner. Each turn costs one bean. If you get knocked out, your beans go to your opponent's handkerchief. This continues until there are no more beans left to play.

The goal is to get all the beans into one team or individual's handkerchief, and the first one to do so is the winner and gets whatever object of value was put in the pot.

CHAPTER 4

THE NAVAJO NATION'S QUEST FOR HARMONY

N avajoland, also known as Diné Bikéyah, covers more than 27,000 square miles (70,000 square km) of stunningly beautiful land that is larger than ten of the fifty American states. It extends into Utah, Arizona, and New Mexico and is distinctive in its ecological diversity. Its scope includes dry, low desert regions, alpine forests with high plateaus, mesas, and mountains. Wind and water erosion, along with volcanic activity, have carved out its characteristically striking canyons, mesas, and mountains. Since time immemorial, the natural world has served to enrich and inform Navajo culture, spirituality, and way of life.

THE DINÉ

The word *Navajo* means "place of large, planted fields" and comes from a different Native American language, called Tewa. Navajo became the name used by the Spanish colonizers who interacted with them. Navajo People actually call themselves the Diné, meaning "the people." It is an Athabaskan word for *man*, but the Navajo routinely use it to refer to themselves and their language. Athabaskan is a language family spoken primarily by Native Americans in Canada, Alaska, and the southwest, and Navajo is part of the southern branch of this language family. It is among the best and most highly documented Native American languages. It was even used as a code language by the United States government during World War II. The complexity of the Navajo language, combined with the fact that there were no published Navajo dictionaries, made it possible to transmit information without being decoded by Japanese or German military forces.

THE POWER OF THE YEI

While the Navajo believe in one Creator who oversees all aspects of life, they also believe in other supernatural beings like Changing Woman, the Monster Slayers, Spider Man, and more. Other Native American Nations believe in similar Holy People, but they are more commonly referred to as Spirits. To the Navajo, they are anthropomorphic deities with supernatural powers called Yei. They each have distinct roles and powers that can be used for both benign and dangerous purposes. This is the highest class of deities, and they can actually be summoned by masked dancers during major Ceremonies. However, those seeking their presence must exercise caution, because depending on their whims or how carefully they are approached, these deities can be either destructive or helpful to humans.

The Navajo relationship to and connection with their homeland is shaped by their Oral Traditions. They believe that the events that occurred from Creation onward took place in specific geographical locations throughout Navajoland. Everything from the birth of Changing Woman, who created the Navajo from her skin, to the slaying of monsters that took place in what are now Arizona, New Mexico, Colorado, and Utah happened in a Navajoland location as opposed to in some ethereal netherworld or within the cosmos. It emphasizes the significance of their landscape because the Navajo believe that when these extraordinary events occurred on Earth they infused the land with power.

THE CHANGING WOMAN

The Navajo believe that Changing Woman left her home in present-day New Mexico and traveled along almost the entirety of the Navajo homeland, stopping at many places along the way. Every time she stopped to rest, she imbued that place with her power, including a set of waterfalls in the Little Colorado River. It is believed that, as a result, it's a good place to stop and offer one's prayers because the inherent power of the place can carry the prayers directly to The Creator. This belief is further reinforced by the way Native Americans experience cyclical time. The Navajo believe that because her journey is stamped onto the land, it is a continually reoccurring event, therefore Changing Woman's power is constantly being absorbed by these specific geographical locations.

THE PROTECTIONWAY

According to the Navajo, the land is a vessel for the Yei's power. No one place is more Sacred than another; instead, they are all bound together in powerful unity. Many Navajo Ceremonies are celebrations of the reciprocal relationship that they have with the land. They give thanks and pay their respects by performing Ceremonies and retelling Oral Traditions like that of Changing Woman's journey. The Protectionway is one such Ceremony, which is performed when someone seeks protection of some kind, either to avoid bad luck or to prevent misfortune, sickness, or other kinds of disasters. The Protectionway siphons its power from the land and delivers it to the person seeking guidance, who chants:

Head of Earth, on the top!
Head of Earth, by your holy power may I also be holy power.
With this power I will be spared.
With this power with which you talk, may I talk.

There are at least sixty major Navajo religious Ceremonies, and most of them involve elaborate combinations of songs, prayers, rituals, sandpainting, and masked dancers. They take place seasonally or when the Navajo require guidance, the Yei's protection, or the restoration of harmony with the supernatural world, as well as the natural world. The most highly revered Navajo Spiritual Leaders are called singers. These are people who know and can perform one or more of the major Navajo Ceremonies in their entirety, from beginning to end. These Spiritual Leaders are more closely akin to priests than Shamans, and gain their knowledge, skills, and techniques through lengthy apprenticeships with already established singers. Known to act as unofficial leaders in their communities, they are deeply respected and highly esteemed.

Haschélti, the Talking God Mask used in the Yebichai Ceremony, also called the Night Chant Ceremony.

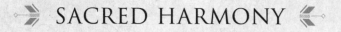

SACRED HARMONY

The ideal of harmony is one you've already heard referenced when it comes to Native Americans' relationships to the planet, their beliefs, and each other. However, it has often been misconstrued or, worse, infantilized. The Navajo believe that those who live in accordance with the universe and all living creatures can expect a clean soul that protects their entire being from evil that could possibly prey upon them.

Harmony, whether achieving harmony within themselves or living harmoniously with the environment, is of great importance to Navajo People. Traditional Navajo wisdom tells us that the way to achieve harmony is through spirituality, also known as Hozho: The Beauty Way of Life. This is possibly more relevant today than it ever was because the foundations of this philosophy emphasize avoiding the separation of secular and spiritual knowledge that is all too common in Western society. It is apparent to the Navajo that there is a connection between this secularization and the many problems that plague contemporary life, and reinforces the importance of this traditional wisdom.

For the Navajo, beauty and harmony are realized when all the forces of the world are in balance, when good overpowers evil, when illness is restored to health, and when order replaces chaos. This state of balance, the Hozho, is the natural condition of the world. That's why in almost every Navajo Ceremony, the phrase "Sa'ah Naaghaii Bik'eh Hohzho"—words that call forth beauty, harmony, and long life—is repeated several times.

Navajo Tradition states that power is generated at the "center" and radiates out to the whole universe. This center can be found anywhere, both physically and metaphorically. It can refer to the center of the mind or body, the center of a Sacred object, the center of a physical structure, or even the universe. This philosophy is applied to all aspects of life—from medical treatments to architecture and textile design.

TRADITIONAL TEXTILE WEAVING

One way in which Navajo People express and seek out harmony is through traditional textile weaving. According to Navajo Creation Oral Traditions, the Diné were led by The Creator from the Under World to Navajoland in the southwest United States. Spider Man taught the Navajo how to make a loom using sunshine, rain, and lightning. Spider Woman taught them to weave as a way to spread the Beauty Way, bringing balance to the mind, body, and soul. Throughout the centuries, Navajo weaving has shifted and evolved depending on their migration patterns, individual needs, improved technology and techniques, contact with other Nations and colonizers, and more. This ranges from thick utility blankets for warmth to extremely splendid blankets meant to be worn as decorative clothing.

When they are first learning their craft, young weavers are told to find a spiderweb first thing in the morning, while it still glistens with sunlight and dew. They are instructed to place the palm of their right hand on the spider's web without hurting or dismantling the web. They believe that it is in that moment that Spider Woman's gift of weaving enters the young person's spirit, where it lives and guides them for the rest of their time on Earth. When weavers create their designs, they work to create a harmonious balance of form and color. When a weaver creates a harmonious design, they are contributing to the overall beauty and goodness of Creation, and in this way, weaving becomes a vessel through which Hozho is expressed.

Often, weavers include a "Spirit Line," which is a small strand of yarn in a contrasting color that trickles through the textile, from the center of the design to the outer edge. Navajo People believe that when they weave, a part of their spirit becomes entwined with the rug. The Spirit Line prevents the weaver's spirit from being trapped in the rug and allows it to safely leave the rug. This practice started in the early 1900s and is still seen today. When traders began requesting that weavers place borders around their designs, traditional Navajo weavers became increasingly concerned about trapping their creative spirits within the weaving, which could possibly hinder their ability to weave down the line. The Spirit Line safely separates the weaver from the weaving, protecting them from any harmful thoughts or experiences that it might come in contact with after it is used or sold. But not all rugs have Spirit Lines. They are most commonly found in rugs with a border (though not all bordered rugs have them). It is up to the weaver's discretion whether they include this deliberate "imperfection."

PRAYER, SONG, AND CHANTS

Like weaving, Navajo songs and words have a generative power. As is the case with many religions, Navajo spirituality places a heavy emphasis on the power of prayer through songs and chants. The difference with Western religions is that Navajo songs themselves are believed to be the spiritual pathway to literal and physical wholeness and healing.

Through prayer, song, and chants, the Navajo can coerce the Yei, their deities, into helping them in whatever way they may need, whether it be with spiritual issues, social problems, or simply to help restore the natural order and balance of society. Many of the chants, prayers, and songs also involve healing. They can be performed during three different kinds of Ceremonies: Lifeway, Evilway, and Holyway.

> » **LIFEWAY CHANTS** are used to heal physical injuries, such as when someone gets hurt while hunting or building. These chants encourage the healing process.

> » **EVILWAY CHANTS** are used to exorcise evil from an individual, the village or community, or the land. The removal of this darkness allows for light to enter once more.

» **HOLYWAY CHANTS** are performed with the intention of attracting virtuosity toward anyone or anything that might need it. These chants are often performed over many nights in an effort to boost their effectiveness. Holyway chants can last anywhere from two to nine nights, with the various parts performed in a specific order.

Others are specifically used to ask the Yei who are manifesting at the ceremony to restore balance and order. The following Navajo chant invokes the beauty of Mythic Time—specifically, the world's original harmony. The chant compels the Yei to become present and restore harmony that has been lost.

The Navajo believe that Thunderbirds represent serenity, bountiful blessings, and an outpouring of happiness. This Navajo chant celebrates and invokes the wondrous beauty of nature and all creatures that inhabit it.

The Earth is beautiful
The Earth is beautiful
The Earth is beautiful
Below, the East, the Earth, its face toward East
The top of its head is beautiful
The soles of its feet, they are beautiful
Its feet, they are beautiful
Its legs, they are beautiful
Its body, it is beautiful
Its chest, it is beautiful
Its head-feather, it is beautiful
The Earth is beautiful

TRADITIONAL NAVAJO SANDPAINTING

Prayer is not the only way that the Navajo invoke the divine. Yei can also be called into being through sandpainting. Like a chant or song, they believe the spirits of deities physically come to them through their sandpaintings, almost acting like a portal for their spiritual forms. It's a powerful, albeit evanescent, form of worship.

Sandpainting is most often used in curative Ceremonies when help is needed for either harvesting or medical healing. This assistance is requested during Ceremonies, and the sandpaintings are the places from which the deities enter and leave the space. Most often, the figures in sandpaintings are symbolic representations of Oral Traditions. They can portray places like the Sacred mountains that are home to the Yei, ancient visions, or even the very dances and chants that are performed during Ceremonies.

Sandpaintings are made from colored sand and pollen and are renowned for their beauty. Because the purpose of the sandpainting is never the finished product, sandpaintings are always ritually destroyed. This helps stop the Yei's power from getting out of control beyond the boundaries of the Ceremony. Sandpaintings' value lies in the very act of creation and in its use for healing. The Navajo also realize that the Yei cannot be held by Earthly forms for long, whether it be via sandpainting or chanting, so they are not sentimentally tied to the individual sandpaintings themselves. The power and value lie in the ephemeral.

An example of a traditional sandpainting pattern.

THE NUMBER FOUR

As we have touched on, a primary principle of Navajo spiritual practice involves maintaining balance and harmony in order to restore the physical health of both the individual and the environment. Another one of the most common fundamentals of Navajo philosophy is the importance of the number four. It permeates all aspects of their spirituality, from the four directions and four seasons to the first four Clans and the four colors that are associated with the four Sacred mountains. This Sacred number represents completeness and mirrors the cyclical nature of time.

There are four seasons, each with its own individual activities and Ceremonies. People's lives are organized via the four directions: north, south, east, and west. Each direction corresponds to one of the four mountains that the Navajo believe the Yei made on the traditional boundaries of Navajoland. They include the north peak of Mount Hesperus in southwestern Colorado (north), the east peak of Mount Blanca in south central Colorado (east), the southern peak of Mount Taylor in New Mexico (south), and the western San Francisco Peaks near Flagstaff, Arizona (west).

Additionally, four colors correspond to each direction, each representing a specific type of stone or shell. Jet represents the color black, which is north; a white shell represents the color white, which is east; turquoise represents the color blue, which is the south; and yellow abalone represents yellow, which is west. Navajo silversmiths can use the four precious stones and shells to connect their work to their spiritual practice. And because Navajo sandpaintings are a way through which one can communicate with the spiritual world, the use of Sacred colors can help deepen the communication while also providing insight into the cultural significance of the work itself. Most sandpaintings consist of four designs placed around the center.

VALUE SYSTEMS

There are four stages in a person's life—childhood, adolescence, early to mid-adulthood, and old age—and there are four values that are all necessary to ensure a whole person and community. They include:

> » **LIFE**—This speaks to the need to maintain positive thoughts while planning one's life, both present and future, as a way to keep the mind sharp.

> » **WORK**—This is a focus on discipline and the commitment to achieving life goals by maintaining productive daily lives via learning, self-care, exercise, and helping others.

> » **SOCIAL AND HUMAN RELATIONSHIPS**—This includes reciprocity, the act of gracefully giving and receiving generosity, helpfulness, acts of kindness, and support, as well as being constantly aware of the interconnectedness between each other, the Spirits, all living creatures, and the universe.

> » **RESPECT AND REVERENCE**—This involves the act of perpetuating faithfulness by respecting oneself, others, nature, animals, and The Creator. It also includes the respect and honoring of The Creator and Yei through prayer, Ceremonies, and the individual's personal spiritual practice.

By keeping these philosophies at the forefront, the Navajo believe they are better equipped to maintain the Hozho ideal.

THE TRADITIONAL NAVAJO HOME

Another way that one can see the significance of the number four reflected in Navajo daily life is through the physical construction of the Traditional Navajo home—a four-post house called the hogan. During Mythic Time, First Man and First Woman breathed life into the four Sacred mountains that define the borders of Navajoland, and the four-posted hogan represents this foundational event. When a Navajo builds a hogan, they follow the same pattern as First Man and First Woman did while forming the four Sacred mountains: They start in the east, then place a post to the south, another to the west, and then the last to the north. This serves as a reminder of origin and place, putting Mythic Time at the center of daily life.

A traditional hogan.

The Blessingway is an Oral Tradition that describes how the first hogan was built for First Man and First Woman by Coyote, a powerful Earth deity, with the help from Beavers, his trusty footmen. This hogan resembled a dome, with five triangular walls. Since the early 1900s, hexagonal or even octagonal hogans have grown in popularity. This new architecture was the result of new construction materials and techniques, though they retained traditional design elements like a circular floor plan and an east-facing door. Generally, all hogans are built with an entrance that faces the east so that a Navajo family will wake and see the rising sun first thing every morning.

Every family must have a traditional hogan for Ceremonies, even if their primary home is more modern. Aside from spiritual reasons, one of the reasons a hogan-style home remains popular among Navajo families is that they are incredibly energy efficient. The use of packed mud against an entirely wood structure means a home is easily kept cool with plenty of air ventilation. Interior fireplaces keep the hogan warm and toasty during the cold winter months.

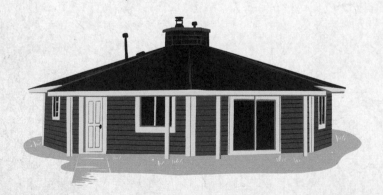

A modern-day hogan.

EVALUATING
YOUR OWN VALUES

Think about your own value systems and consider the following questions:

» What are your value systems? Do you have a strong sense of justice? Are you a vegetarian for ethical purposes? Do you reject the act of stealing or killing another under any circumstance? Make a list of the top five values that you live by.

» If you were raised in a different culture, do you believe these values might be different or similar?

» If you were raised in a different religion or spiritual practice, how do you believe these values would change?

» If your systems were challenged by an unexpected situation, how do you think they might be subject to change?

» Consider the value systems of the Navajo People. Do any of your own value systems align, and if so, how?

CHAPTER 5

THE CHEROKEE NATION AND THE LAND OF BLUE SMOKE

The Cherokee are one of the largest Native American Nations, with more than 430,000 members, consisting of three Tribes with a common language, culture, and heritage. Until the late 1700s, they were one united Tribe, sharing an ancestral homeland spanning states in southern Appalachia and the southeast, including North Carolina, Georgia, Alabama, and southern Tennessee. Their division is the result of one of the most painful chapters in American history: the Trail of Tears. The United Keetoowah Band of Cherokee were the first of the Cherokee to leave and move west, prior to the forced removal. The Cherokee Nation is made up of those who survived the death march and live on Cherokee land in Oklahoma. The Eastern Band of Cherokee Indians were those who hid or escaped the Trail of Tears and went back to their homeland in North Carolina. We will take a deeper look at the Trail of Tears later in this chapter.

THE PEOPLE
OF THE LAND OF BLUE SMOKE

The Cherokee flag is adorned with the Cherokee Nation seal, which is surrounded by seven stars representing the seven Clans, and an additional black star in remembrance of all those who died as a result of the Trail of Tears, which we will discuss in greater detail later in the chapter. The seal itself was created as a result of an executive Act that was passed under Chief Lewis Downing in 1869. The Act called for the seal to include a seven-pointed star inside a wreath of oak leaves, which symbolizes the eternal flame and resilience of the Cherokee People. The points of the star represent the seven traditional Cherokee Clans.

The Cherokee call their ancestral homelands Shaconage, the Land of Blue Smoke. Now known as the Great Smoky Mountains that rise along the borders of Tennessee and North Carolina, they are a part of the Blue Ridge Mountain System. This area gets its name from the bluish haze that can arise from aerosols in the area that cause short wavelengths of bluish light to scatter. It is now a National Park, and more than ten million visitors a year come to bask in the wonder of the lush, still-flourishing, verdant hills and cascading waterfalls of Great Smoky Mountains National Park.

The Cherokee put great stock in and are incredibly proud of their resilience. And even though a majority of Cherokee People today practice some denomination of Christianity, a significant number still observe and practice older Traditions, despite all of the hardships they have endured. They meet at Ceremonial grounds and practice Stomp Dances and perform other Ceremonies. These Traditional Ceremonies are considered Sacred and are not open to the public. The Cherokee have seven major Ceremonies, many of which go on for several days. They often take place around the new moon, and can include fasting, dancing, feasting, purification rites, and more. These Ceremonies offer opportunities for the community to come together to bond with each other and worship, and are generally a joyful time. Musical instruments like drums, gourd rattles, and turtle-shell rattles are used for dancing and festivals. Storytelling and stickball games are other means of exuberant expressions of thanks that take place during these cyclical ceremonies.

THE UKU DANCE

While most of these Ceremonies follow the cycles of the seasons or the moon, the Uku Dance Ceremony is celebrated only once every seven years. *Uku* is the Cherokee word for Chief, and this Ceremony is not only a chance for Clan members to acknowledge and honor the principal Chief but also serves to remind the Cherokee of their one true Chief—The Creator. During this Ceremony, the Cherokee Chief is carried into the Sacred Circle and acknowledged. Usually held in winter, the Uku is given new clothing and dances are done in his honor.

The Uku Dance Ceremony, like all the festivals that make up the yearly religious cycle of the Cherokee, is a vital time to connect with themselves, the community, and their heritage. By sharing stories, praying, feasting, and dancing, they remember and honor the Traditions of the Elders and keep their culture present and alive.

THE GREEN CORN CEREMONY AND THE STOMP DANCE

Another celebration, the Green Corn Ceremony, is one of the Cherokee's most important spiritual and social events. Held during the late summer harvest, it is a time of thanksgiving, renewal, and forgiveness. It gives members of the community the opportunity to wipe the slate clean, both between themselves and The Creator and with other members of the community with whom they have had discord or have harmed. It is during this Ceremony that the famous Cherokee Stomp Dances are performed—an event that is equal parts exciting and meditative.

The fact that this celebration takes place to this day is a testament to the strength and courage of the Cherokee People, who have worked diligently to preserve their culture and lands, all the while honoring those who came before them and those who will come after them. They remain committed to preserving and promoting Cherokee language and values, protecting their inherent sovereignty, and working to improve the quality of life for the next seven generations of Cherokee Nation citizens.

Stomp Dances are Ceremonies that are imbued with both religious and social significance. It is most often affiliated with the Green Corn Ceremony, though it can be performed during other Ceremonies as well. Corn, quite possibly the single most important food for the Cherokee, played an important part in their religious and ceremonial life. The Green Corn Ceremony was a thanksgiving Ceremony generally held after the harvest to celebrate the renewal of life, the corn crop, and the community at large. It was performed when the new corn was ripe enough to eat, and no new corn could be eaten until after the Ceremony had concluded. The Cherokee also considered it a time of forgiveness, and sought to move past community resentments like debts, love affairs, old grudges, and even crimes. It is one of the important major Ceremonies to have survived centuries of colonialism and attempted genocide.

On the first day of the Ceremony, the community would gather for opening rituals, which began with a big feast as a way to prepare for the impending period of fasting. Fasting lasted one to two days, with strict observance among men, but with leniency for women, children, and the elderly, who could eat certain foods at specific, preordained times. In keeping with the theme of renewal, men would work together to repair and update community buildings, while women worked to clean and tidy their private homes, repairing clothing, utensils, and tools as needed.

The important public events took place in the middle of the ceremonial grounds, including various dances by men and women, and speeches that were given by Elders of the community imploring everyone to forgive past transgressions and move into the future mindfully. The rekindling of the Sacred Fire was another very important element of the Green Corn Ceremony. The Cherokee believed that over the course of the year, the Sacred Fire was contaminated and corrupted whenever people transgressed against each other or society and therefore needed to be renewed. In order to achieve this, the Cherokee would extinguish all the fires in the community and clean their own hearths at home. Afterwards, the Sacred Fire is once again lit, and used to relight all the other fires in the community. It is a time to celebrate a fresh, clean start and new beginnings. This is followed by celebratory games and dances, including the Stomp Dance.

Often the conclusion of a celebration, the Stomp Dance is a lively group dance for both men and women. The dance symbolizes the dispersal of the Sacred Fire given to the Keetoowah People by The Creator and the Thunder Beings in Mythic Time. The men sing Stomp Dance songs in a call-and-answer style, with one man as the leader and the rest of the men as the chorus. The dancers carry handheld turtle-shell rattles, while women provide the rhythm with shakers worn around their legs and ankles, creating a vibrant cacophony of sound. The women carrying the shakers fall in step behind the song leader, while the remaining dancers follow in a counterclockwise spiral around the Sacred Fire. Each individual dance continues until at least four songs, or four rounds, are accomplished by the chosen dance leader. There is usually a short five-minute break between dance leaders, giving dancers a time to rest and recuperate throughout the long night of revelry.

Depending on the number of people in the community, up to several hundred people may join the dance circle. It is not meant to be a grueling event, but a celebratory one, and almost everyone at the Ceremonial grounds dances throughout the night. It's no wonder that ethnomusicologist Victoria Lindsay Levine wrote, "Stomp Dance songs are among the most exhilarating and dramatic musical genres in Native America."

There are many protections in place to ensure not only that the people participating in the Ceremonies remain safe, but also that channels of communication with The Creator, the Spirits, and the people remain open, positive, and untainted. Participants and visitors cannot use drugs or alcohol while there and, depending on the Ceremony , they also cannot have had either for a specific length of time before or after the dance. Photography of any kind is not allowed at Ceremonial dances, and oftentimes participants do not feel comfortable discussing specific details of the Ceremonies with non-Natives. Pregnant or menstruating women are not to enter the dance circle at Ceremonial grounds, though they may observe. There are many active Ceremonial Stomp Grounds on current Native land, including Stokes Smith Stomp Dance Ground on Cherokee Nation land, and Eastern Band Cherokee Stomp Grounds in Raven's Roost, North Carolina.

THE THREE CONNECTED WORLDS

The foundation of the Cherokee religion is based in the belief that the universe was made of three connected worlds: the Middle World, the Upper World, and the Under World.

The Middle World is where they, we, and all living beings and spirits reside. The Cherokee believed the Earth was a flat disk of water with a large island floating in the middle, and that our planet hung by four cords—one in the north, east, south, and west—from a sky arch made of stone. Above the sky arch was the Upper World, where the guiding and protective spirits of ancestors and animals that had passed away lived. These spirits could move from the Upper World to the Middle World and back again as necessary to help humankind maintain peace and harmony on Earth. Below the Earth was the Under World of bad spirits that brought chaos and disaster. They could soar upwards to the Middle World through lakes, caves, and deep springs to cause trouble and disrupt the harmonious balance of things.

THE BALANCE OF NATURE

Like other Native cultures, the Cherokee have never seen themselves as separate from their environment. They do not try to dominate or control nature; they simply seek to keep their own proper place within it. They believe that everything in the environment has an intelligent spirit, and this belief plays a central role not only in Cherokee Oral Traditions but in their daily practices as well. A profound respect for their surroundings influences everything from how they harvest medicines to hunting animals for food. For example, Cherokee conservation practices dictated that when they gathered medicinal plants out in the forest, they harvested only every fourth one they found, so that the other three could grow without interference for future use.

Practices such as this contributed to the stability of the world, and the Cherokee believed that if the balance of nature was upset, it could result in sickness, poor crops, war, and more. It was the responsibility of humans to keep harmony with each other, animals, nature, and within their own selves. They turned to the guiding and protective spirits of the Upper World to help keep balance and harmony on Earth, both by providing guidance and support and by interfering when humans needed help overcoming the havoc caused by spirits from the Under World. The Cherokee also maintained balance by practicing daily prayers, rituals, and seasonal ceremonies.

There are seven key Cherokee values, and they consider them to be the guiding tent poles that have enabled them to remain resilient and survive centuries of colonialism as well as other hardships. These tenets shape every aspect of the culture and way of life, from how they imbue their spirituality into their daily routines to how they connect with and uplift members of their communities.

KEY VALUE SYSTEMS

According to the Cherokee Preservation Foundation, key Cherokee values, past and present, include:

» SPIRITUALITY—Members of the Cherokee Nation cherish the bond they have with the Spiritual world and consider it one of the main common threads that unites their community. It is a beacon of hope through both good and bad times.

» **Group harmony in community and family relationships**—Maintaining serenity and harmony within immediate and wider relationships can be ensured by generously sharing and giving of one's time, talent, and resources without resentment.

» **Strong individual character**—Cherokee People are encouraged to cultivate, nurture, and develop a powerful sense of self, prioritizing integrity, honesty, perseverance, courage, respect, trust, honor, and humility.

» **Strong connection with the land**—This includes not only honoring and preserving the land where they live but also fostering a commitment to the stewardship of the homelands.

» **Honoring the past**—This can be achieved by actively learning about and knowing one's ancestors, identifying with and being active in the Tribe, and living the Cherokee way as a means of preserving the culture.

» **Educating the children**—This includes not only teaching them about their histories and cultural practices but also emphasizing the importance of these core values in every aspect of their lives. One of the most important ways to do so is by being strong role models for them.

» **Possessing a sense of humor**—The Cherokee believe that having a lighthearted outlook on life and a sense of humor about themselves and the world can help ease pressure during intense situations and in turn help people make good decisions.

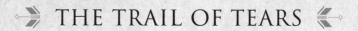

THE TRAIL OF TEARS

You may have been introduced to the Cherokee by way of learning about the Trail of Tears, one of the most shameful events in the United States' history. One cannot discuss Cherokee culture and practices without also acknowledging this significant event, which changed the course of the Cherokee Nation's history and laid the foundation for the community that they are today.

The Trail of Tears was the forced, brutal relocation of what was likely around 100,000 people belonging to the Cherokee, Creek, Chickasaw, Choctaw, and Seminole Nations to what is now Cherokee territory in Oklahoma. Congress, led by President Andrew Jackson, wanted access to the gold and land that rightfully belonged to these Native American Nations. President Jackson passed the Indian Removal Act in 1830, and the Cherokee did their best to resist this decision by every means possible for the better part of the decade that followed. They lobbied Congress, sent their young men on speaking tours through the country to educate non-Native Americans on the issue, and created a petition with more than 15,000 Cherokee signatures. Junaluska, a Cherokee leader who had actually saved President Jackson's life at the Battle of Horseshoe Bend, attempted to appeal to the president for mercy directly, but Jackson refused to see him. They even took their case to the Supreme Court and won, with the court ruling that they were a sovereign Nation.

Despite all of this, President Andrew Jackson ignored the decision, enforced the Indian Removal Act of 1830, and signed the Treaty of New Echota, which gave the Cherokee five million dollars and land in present-day Oklahoma in exchange for their seven million acres of ancestral land. On December 29, 1935, a small group of about

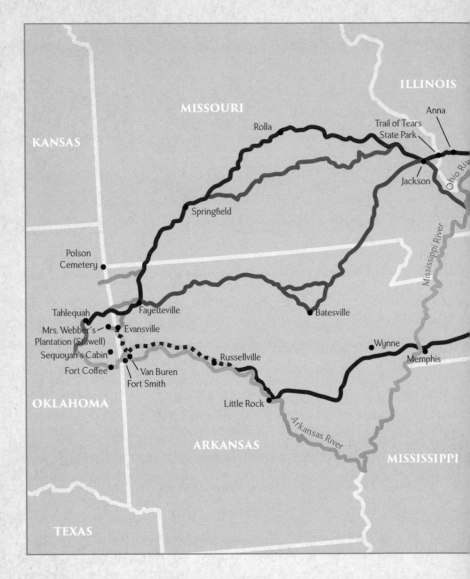

A map showing the different routes various Tribal Nations walked during
their forced relocation from their ancestral lands to government-sanctioned
territory in what is now Oklahoma. Collectively, they are known as the
Trail of Tears.

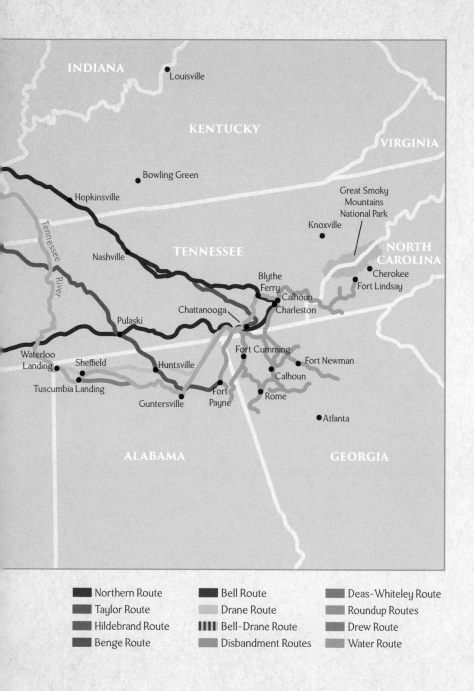

INDIANA

Louisville

KENTUCKY

VIRGINIA

Bowling Green

Hopkinsville

Great Smoky
Mountains
National Park

Knoxville

Tennessee

Nashville

TENNESSEE

NORTH
CAROLINA

River

Blythe
Ferry

Cherokee
Fort Lindsay

Chattanooga

Calhoun

Pulaski

Charleston

Waterloo
Landing

Sheffield

Huntsville

Fort Cumming

Fort Newman

Calhoun

Tuscumbia Landing

Guntersville

Fort
Payne

Rome

Atlanta

ALABAMA

GEORGIA

◼ Northern Route
◼ Taylor Route
◼ Hildebrand Route
◼ Benge Route

◼ Bell Route
◼ Drane Route
|||| Bell-Drane Route
◼ Disbandment Routes

◼ Deas-Whiteley Route
◼ Roundup Routes
◼ Drew Route
◼ Water Route

500 Cherokee individuals who claimed to represent the Nation signed this treaty, despite the vast majority of Cherokee people being strongly opposed. To this day, this is considered a shocking act of betrayal, and three of these people were in fact assassinated by other Cherokee in 1839. The treaty was ratified by Congress in 1836, and the government began constructing stockades to prepare for the removal.

In 1838, the Cherokee People were forcibly taken from their homes, incarcerated in stockades, beaten, tortured, and forced to walk 1,200 miles (1,931 km) by United States government authorities. The march lasted six months and more than 4,000 people died of disease, starvation, and exhaustion during this horrific journey. Many are buried in unmarked graves along the route that is now known as the Trail of Tears. During the removal, about 300 to 400 Cherokee people hid in the densely wooded mountains in western North Carolina. Altogether, about 1,000 Cherokees, including those who hid, made their way back from the Trail of Tears to their ancestral lands. They are the ancestors of our current-day Eastern Band of Cherokee Indians, a sovereign Nation with more than 14,000 members.

You cannot study Cherokee spirituality without also discussing the impact of the Trail of Tears. This is in large part due to the fact that the Cherokee do not see a separation between the spiritual and physical realms of existence. To be removed from their physical lands was just as much an assault on their spiritual life as it was on their homes and bodies. Those who survived passed their physical and spiritual resilience down to their descendants, and the experience has shaped every aspect of their spiritual lives.

FINDING BALANCE

Finding balance is a key tenet of many religions, including Taoism, Hinduism, and Buddhism. Balance can be found in ways big and small, from respecting yourself and others in the face of adversity to keeping your desk organized and clean so you can focus on your work.

> What are three things you can do on a daily basis to help ensure that your life remains balanced? Try one every day for a week and see how it affects your daily routines, mindset, and stress levels.

Keep in mind this excerpt from a traditional Cherokee prayer:

Peace and happiness are available in every moment.
Peace is every step. We shall walk hand in hand.
There are no political solutions to spiritual problems.
Remember: if The Creator put it there, it is in the right place.
The soul would have no rainbow if the eyes had no tears.

CHAPTER 6

THE SACRED SALMON FEAST AND THE CHINOOK NATION

The Chinook Nation is made up of the five westernmost Chinook-speaking Bands, another term for individual groups of Chinook People, at the mouth of the Columbia River, the largest river system in the Pacific Northwest. These Bands include the Lower Chinook, Clatsop, Wahkiakum, Cathlamet, and Willapa. The Clatsop and Cathlamet reside in Oregon, while the Lower Chinook, Wahkiakum, and Willapa reside in Washington State. The gloomy rain and chilly, often foggy, climate of the area has deeply influenced their spirituality. They are very attuned to the workings of the Spirits in nature and pay heed to signs that might otherwise go unnoticed to the untrained eye.

FEDERAL RECOGNITION

As they did with many other Native Americans, the United States government tried to remove the Chinook from their homeland, but they refused to sign a treaty that would have forced them to lose their land. They remain on the lands of their ancestors to this day, making them one of few Native American Nations that was never moved to a reservation. However, this has had its consequences.

Federal recognition is incredibly important to Native American Nations because it acknowledges their sovereignty and grants them access to federal and state resources that can be put towards funding housing, public health, and education. Despite being formally recognized toward the end of the Clinton administration more than twenty years ago, this status was rescinded just eighteen months later by the Bush administration. This could be seen as long-standing retribution for having refused to sign the Chehalis River Treaty in 1855—the aforementioned treaty that would have moved them from their ancestral land to a reservation. All of the other Native American Nations who signed the treaty currently have federal recognition. Many members of the Chinook Nation have likened their lack of federal recognition to a "slow genocide," as they are cut off from resources that they desperately need, especially regarding public health.

Despite decades of litigation, petitions, congressional legislations, and personal appeals to sitting presidents, they remain unrecognized. Having to move through so many levels of impersonal red tape and dispassionate bureaucracy not only wastes precious time, but it also hides the urgency and pain that the Chinook feel as time continues to move on without this important designation. Children fall behind in their education timelines, the elderly go without the medical care they need, and a lack of infrastructure and support makes it difficult for people to work, exacerbating a cycle of poverty for many. The Covid-19 pandemic has only served to further highlight this disparity, as there has been no social safety net in any way, from a lack of government financial aid to being unable to get access to vaccines and medicine for the community. The consequences of this are far-reaching and permeate every facet of modern Chinook life, but they remain undeterred, and they continue to fight for recognition and resources they desperately need and deserve.

A traditional depiction of an eagle for the Chinook-speaking Bands of the Pacific Northwest.

THE CHINOOK CREATION ORAL TRADITION

The Chinook have considered Saddle Mountain in Oregon as their place of origin since Mythic Time. The Chinook's Creation Oral Tradition occurs there, and recounts how the first men came from the sky. They were the offspring of Thunderbird—part man, part Spirit—who had laid eggs on Saddle Mountain. A giantess rolled five of these eggs down the mountain into the valley, after which five men were born from them. They made up the first Chinook Tribe. In the valley, the men found women in various stages of development, and the Chief plucked his wife from a rock. Her arms went through it as if she had been hugging it, and to this day there is a rock with this feature in the Pacific Northwest.

The Chinook Creation Oral Tradition also states that before The Creator gave humans life, He called a Grand Council of all the animals and plants, asking each to bestow a gift on the new helpless humans that would enable them to survive. The very first to come forward and offer their services was Salmon, who selflessly offered his body to feed people. Secondly, Water came forward, promising to be Salmon's home. While everyone else at the Council also offered the humans a gift, it is most significant that the very first two were Salmon and Water. To honor that sacrifice, these two have a place of honor at all traditional feasts. The Ceremonies begin with blessing and drinking of water, followed by a prayer of thanksgiving for the salmon that is being served. The Ceremony fortifies the vital role that salmon and water play in the health, culture, and well-being of the Chinook People. After the blessings, the foods are honored and eaten, the more solemn portion of the Ceremony concludes, and the event becomes a jubilant, festive occasion for all to enjoy.

Like all Native Americans, the geography of the land on which the Chinook live heavily influenced their lifestyle. As a result of surrendering themselves and adapting to the environment at large, all of their needs were met. Because of the wet weather, the natural resources of the northwest coast were abundant. The densely wooded forests of the area provided cedar wood (which was soft and easy to carve) for large longhouses that several families could occupy at once. These structures were organized into villages that could accommodate and support as many as 1,000 people. Cedar wood was also used to build remarkably designed, massive, and ornate canoes, the traditional method of transportation.

A cedar tree, one of the four Sacred Herbs.

THE CANOE JOURNEY

Members of the Chinook Nation still participate in what is known as the Canoe Journey, an inter-Tribal event that is considered to be a profound and meaningful cultural experience. Each year, a different Nation hosts, with participants from Indigenous canoe families from all over the world, including Aotearoa, Hawai'i, Alaska, and more. The Heiltsuk Nation of Bella Bella, British Columbia, travel the longest distance each year, by canoe only, which can take up to a month.

The Canoe Journey starts with one family, who sets out and paddles to the nearest neighbor to camp out for the night. Once there, they sing and dance for their hosts. The next day, more canoe families gather to paddle to the next neighbor, asking for permission to come ashore and camp, sing, and dance for the hosts. The next day, the Protocol is continued with even more families. Once everyone reaches the final landing in the Host Tribe's territory, there can be more than 100 canoe families traveling together. There they camp for a week to rest and celebrate with old friends. The Host Tribe provides meals, camping space, laundry, and facilities for what could be thousands of people. As a means of thanks, each canoe family sings, dances, and brings gifts for the Host Tribe. On the last day of the gathering, the Host Tribe hosts a Potlatch, a large, Ceremonial feast, concluding the celebration with songs, dances, and gifts for all the participants.

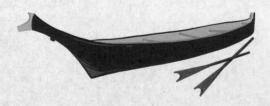

The Chinook canoe features a raised prow that is generally decorated with ornate carved figures. They are brilliantly handcrafted and range from 15 to 50 feet (4.5 to 15 m) in length. Made for use in both fresh and salt water, these canoes were fashioned by hollowing out a single log, usually from a western red cedar. Before the Chinook had access to metal tools, this was done through fires and steam, making it an incredibly slow process. A high-quality canoe could take several weeks to make, and consequently was highly valued.

Also known as the Nootka canoe, the Chinook canoe could carry and transport many people. It was also used to haul goods up and down the coastline for trade and other purposes. Chinook canoes are so impressive that members of the Lewis and Clark expedition stole one from the Chinook Nation. It was only recently returned to its rightful community.

THE POTLATCH CEREMONY

You are likely familiar with the word and concept of a potluck—a communal meal where guests bring food to share. There are many who believe its roots lie in the Potlatch Ceremony and celebration. The Potlatch is one of the most common Chinook traditions, a Ceremony where one family redistributes their wealth among the community. The host gives away their possessions both as a way to demonstrate their wealth (though they would normally get most of these back in future Potlatches held by others) and to foster a sense of camaraderie within Chinook society. The more the host gave away, the more honor and social status they achieve. This generosity and gift-giving is a core principle of the Chinook People and highlights the importance of lending each other a helping hand.

Alongside gift-giving, the Ceremony also involved dancing, music, extravagant feasts, and honoring The Creator and the Spirits. The music and dancing were representative of the joy they feel as a result of the many blessings bestowed on them by The Creator. Potlatches were performed for all manner of occasions, including rites of passage, births, weddings, building new Clan homes, funerals, and honoring the deceased.

The Potlatch was one of several Native American Ceremonies banned in Canada. It was outlawed from 1885 until 1951. Missionaries and other officials saw that this Ceremony was the heart of the Indigenous cultural system, therefore putting it in direct conflict with their colonialist agenda. Aside from the obvious motivations for this particular kind of spiritual oppression, it also further served the Canadian colonizer narrative that the Chinook and other Native

Americans who practiced Potlatch were "not stable." Why else would someone give away all their earthly possessions unless they were deeply unwell? It was deemed "unstable" behavior and banned for the better part of a century.

For the most part, the Chinook were able to circumvent or flat out ignore this law, holding underground celebrations. And though the ban was mainly ineffective, it did cause significant cultural damage and erasure. Once it was lifted and the Chinook were able to openly practice Potlatch again, there was a widespread revival that gained prominence, especially during the 1970s and 1980s, and continues today.

Cultural events like these are meaningful because, like all the other Native American Nations we've discussed thus far, the Chinook's relationship with other members of their community is informed by their spiritual beliefs. Keeping old practices alive that honor their Traditional ways helps their communities at large keep their relationship to The Creator alive and present. The Potlatch is another example of the cultural and spiritual significance of community gatherings.

THE FEAST
OF THE SALMON

The First Salmon Feast is generally considered to be one of the Chinook Nation's most popular and important Ceremonies. The Chinook regard salmon to be Sacred martyrs who sacrifice themselves knowingly to sustain and nourish human life. There is also the belief that a salmon is immortal, and once it is consumed it is reconstituted in a human form and lives in a house under the ocean. It is the Elders of the community that teach the younger ones that salmon, along with deer, elk, root vegetables, and berries, are their brothers and sisters and should be treated as such—with much respect and gentle care. Even as they eat the salmon, the Chinook People treat it with great honor, because it is sent to them from the Great Spirit. The First Salmon Feast Ceremony takes place before open fishing can begin.

At the start of the Ceremony, women go to the south side and men to the north side of the longhouse, with each group forming a circle that stands shoulder to shoulder. Drummers beat a sequence of prayer songs while the community Leaders ring a brass bell as a means to count the song sequences. The songs thank the salmon for its sacrifice and serve as a reminder to all that are gathered of the importance of Traditional Laws being observed. While the songs are being performed, the food is brought out for the assembled group. Young men serve salmon, deer, and other meats, while young women serve huckleberries, roots, and bread. Before everyone starts to eat, the Leader rings the bell again and sings out the Chinook word for water: "choosh." This signals to the participants to have a drink of water, after which the food can be eaten. At the closing of the meal, after the last song is sung, the Leader calls out "choosh" once more, and everyone has a final drink of water.

Historically, First Salmon Ceremonies have always differed slightly among the various Tribes, but they also have many things in common, like how the Chief selects one fisherman to catch the first salmon—a huge honor that requires a blessing or purification rite beforehand. Once that fish was caught, it would be prepared and distributed to the community in a manner unique to the specific location and the individual Tribe. The head of the fish remained pointing upriver to show the salmon's spirit the way home, and the bones would be carefully cleaned and returned to the river, where it was believed the salmon would restore itself and continue on its journey.

In the United States, all farm-raised salmon are Atlantic salmon, which is a different species than Chinook salmon from the Pacific Northwest. Chinook salmon are the largest species of Pacific salmon and can grow as long as 4.9 feet (1.5 m) and up to 129 pounds (58.5 kg)—practically as big as an adult human. Most, however, are in the range of about 3 feet (1 m) and 30 pounds (14 kg), which is still more than enough to satisfy a crowd.

CHINOOK HORN CARVINGS AND BURIAL CANOES

Unlike the Haida, Tlingit, Tsimshian, Kwakwaka'wakw (Kwakiutl), Nuxalk (Bella Coola), and Nuu-chah-nulth (Nootka), their neighbors to the North, the Chinook did not carve totem poles. They did, however, make horn carvings for everything from valued aesthetic art to everyday utilitarian objects like utensils. They used animal horns to create bowls with complex geometric patterns or animal shapes. They would also make sculptures out of antlers or bone. These days, Chinook People still make horn carvings to create masterful works of art. It is a powerful way to reconnect with and honor their culture while also elevating Chinook visibility outside of their own community.

In the past, Chinookan communities would appoint members of their community to specific professions, and that included the occupation of artisanry. It was their job to create artistic objects from wood, bone, stone, antlers, and horns every day. Canoes were bedecked with artistic elements that gave them symbolic power and increased their worth. Both animal and human characteristics were represented, sometimes via geometrical shapes and patterns or skeletal features. Important numbers, like three and five, and mirror imagery are also prevalent in these artistic carvings. Paint was used on occasion to

A spoon carved from a horn.

indicate that the artisan who made the object—or the person who had commissioned it—had high social status, with black representing the Earth and red symbolizing the ancestors. Some carved objects like wealth posts and burial canoes served very specific spiritual purposes.

RITE OF PASSAGE

Death was considered a rite of passage for survivors just as much as it was for those who had passed on. Canoe burial was the preferred method of internment for the Chinook People. Once the body was washed and clothed by specialists, it would lie in state for several days in their home. Mourners would cut their hair and fast, singing elegies in the morning and evening. After this period, the body would be wrapped and placed in a canoe, which was placed on a platform by the river or on rocks. At times, the burial canoes were suspended from trees, up to 8 feet (2.4 m) from the ground. Holes were made in the bottom of the canoe, both for the purpose of letting out rain and to prevent it from being used again by anyone living.

Grave goods were placed inside or surrounding the outside of the canoe and included only the deceased Chinook individual's personal items. For men, this included a bow and arrow, guns, paddles, or jewelry. Women's items were hung on the outside of the canoe, often on poles, and included kitchen utensils, wooden bowls, kettles, pans, baskets, and blankets. The Chinook believed that the dead revisited the Earth at night and would become very angry if they saw their things being used by others, which is why these items were buried with them. If the person who had died was of high social status or wealthy, often a second canoe would be placed on top and bound to the first to create an enclosed coffin of sorts. These were then placed in cemeteries and buried entirely.

ROASTED SALMON
WITH BLUEBERRY SAUCE

You can access Chinook salmon if you happen to be in the region and make your own version of the Chinook's delicious feast. As an alternative, you can use whatever variety of salmon is available to you and enjoy flavors and ingredients that call to mind the essence of the Chinook People's most treasured meal.

Ingredients:

For the salmon:

1 pound (450 g) salmon fillet

1 tablespoon olive oil

Salt and pepper, to taste

1 lemon, sliced, plus extra wedges for serving

1 tablespoon capers

1 small handful rosemary sprigs

Seasonal vegetable, to serve (optional)

For the sauce:

1 tablespoon olive oil

¼ cup (38 g) finely chopped onion

1 clove garlic, minced

1½ cups (285 g) blueberries (fresh or frozen)

2 tablespoons balsamic vinegar

1 tablespoon brown sugar

1 teaspoon grated fresh ginger

1 teaspoon grated lemon zest

Salt and pepper, to taste

Directions:

1. **To make the salmon:** Preheat the oven to 425°F (220°C) and place a piece of baking parchment or foil on a baking tray.

2. Brush the salmon fillet with the olive oil, then season with salt and pepper. Place half of the lemon slices on the tray, then lay the salmon, skin side down, on top. Scatter the capers and remaining lemon slices over the salmon, then lay the sprigs of rosemary on top of the dressed salmon. Roast for 12 to 15 minutes, until the internal temperature of the fish reaches 120°F (50°C).

3. **As the salmon cooks, make the sauce:** In a small skillet, heat the olive oil over medium heat. Add the onion and garlic and cook, stirring frequently, for 2 to 3 minutes. Add the blueberries, vinegar, brown sugar, ginger, and lemon zest, bring to a boil, then reduce the heat to a simmer. Allow the mixture to simmer for 12 to 15 minutes, until the sauce has reduced to approximately 1 cup (240ml) liquid.

4. When the sauce and salmon are done, remove the rosemary sprigs from atop the salmon and place the cooked fillet on a plate. Pour the sauce over the salmon and season with salt and pepper. Serve alongside some lemon wedges and a seasonal vegetable of your choice, if you like.

CHAPTER 7

THE PEOPLE OF THE GREAT LAKES: THE CHIPPEWA NATION

Also known as the Ojibwe (also spelled Ojibwa or Ojibway), the Chippewa Nation is one of the largest Native American Nations, with 150 different Bands located throughout their ancestral homelands in Minnesota, Wisconsin, North Dakota, and Michigan, as well as southern Canada. They are known as the People of the Great Lakes and reside primarily around the region of Lake Superior, above Michigan's Upper Peninsula. Despite this, the Chippewa believe that they actually originated on the North American east coast and then traveled west by various routes to the Great Lakes area because of a series of prophecies known as the Seven Fires, which we will revisit in more detail later in the chapter.

WHO ARE THE CHIPPEWA PEOPLE?

Depending on the areas where they live, some Bands prefer to be known as Chippewa, while others reject it outright and go by Ojibwe. Chippewa is considered to be the attempted pronunciation of early French explorers, but there are a large number of Bands in the States that embrace the name. For the purposes of clarity, we'll be referring to them as the Chippewa Nation unless discussing a specific Band, in which case they will be referred to by their own preference. In general, Canadian Bands prefer Ojibwe and Native American Bands in the United States use Chippewa, as it is the name that has been used in all treaties and technically remains the official name. In their language, they refer to themselves as Anishinaabe, meaning "The Original People." The word *Ojibwe* is an Algonquian word that means "to roast until puckered up," and was likely a reference to the puckered seam of the moccasins they wore.

For the Chippewa-Cree, an independent Nation made up of both Chippewa and Cree Native Americans, the Sweet Grass Hills are an important part of their spirituality, shaping their Traditions for thousands of years. The Sweet Grass Hills are a small group of low mountains in Montana with three conical buttes that can be seen for more than a hundred miles. The Chippewa-Cree believe that these hills are where The Creator began remaking the world after the Great Flood, which took place during Mythic Time. They also say that when the buffalo were obliterated by settlers in the nineteenth century, they descended into a large cave in the Hills' West Butte—a belief reinforced by the fact that these Hills were one of the last areas where buffalo were found before their catastrophic end. It remains a place of great spiritual significance and reverence.

CEREMONIES AND BELIEFS

The Chippewa have a variety of Ceremonies and beliefs that are considered vital components to their culture and spirituality. A key value in Chippewa society includes walking in harmony with the world, connected to all parts of the land with no separation between the Sacred and the secular. All creatures have spirits—from plants to animals, the Earth, and people. This endows their many daily activities with spiritual significance, and seemingly normal routines are interwoven with aspects of worship. The Chippewa call the spirits Manitous, or mysteries. They are the sources of life and existence. Whether it be to The Creator or invocation of the Manitous, Chippewa prayer takes many forms, but during special Ceremonies it is often accompanied by smoke, drums, singing, and dancing.

Like many Native Nations, the Chippewa honor and revere their Elders, who are respected for their wisdom and knowledge. And while they are a patrilineal society, women are also highly respected, upheld as the bearers of life and protectors of water.

The Chippewa put great stock in dreams, and it is from their Oral Traditions that the Dream Catcher came to pass. They do not believe dreams occur in their bodies or minds, but that their souls actually experience the events in their dreams. As a result, dreams are essential to understanding not only their inner lives but also what their future holds. Dreams are considered a twin experience to that of a vision quest, which all Chippewa People undergo at various points in their lives, for a variety of reasons. Through fasting and self-deprivation, they bring on visions and dreams that provide them with knowledge on everything from healing to self-awareness.

Like all Nations, Traditional Chippewa moccasins were designed for their specific environment. They were made from readily available materials like animal skins and often featured intricate embroidery and beadwork. These soft-soled moccasins often had floral elements on the top, the vamp, and cuffs.

THE SEVEN FIRES PROPHECY

An important component of the Chippewa Creation Oral Tradition is the Seven Fires Prophecy. It tells the story of the Nation's migration to their current lands from the eastern American coast, during which seven prophets came during seven fires. The prophecies stated that they would stop seven times to create villages along their journey, but the journey would not be complete until they were led to the place where wild rice, which they call manoomin, grows.

The First Prophet warned that if the Chippewa did not move from their current land by the sea, there would be much suffering and destruction. He shared that they would come upon a turtle-shaped island at the beginning and the end of their journey, and that they would know they had reached the chosen ground when they found the "food that grows on water"—wild rice.

The Second Prophet told them that they would recognize the Second Fire when they were camped by a large body of water that they called the sweet water sea. He warned that the Chippewa would lose their way, both spiritually and physically, and that a young boy would be born to help point them back in the direction of the Traditional ways and the path that leads to the stepping-stones of their future.

The Third Prophet said that in the Third Fire they would find the path that led to the lands that were prepared to continue on their journey west to the place where the food grows upon the water.

The Fourth Prophet was two beings who came as one and warned of the coming of a light-skinned race. The first of the two said that the future of their people would be determined by whether or not the light-skinned race came bearing the face of brotherhood. If they did, there would be a time of wonderful change and unity, with new knowledge being joined with old knowledge that would help create a mighty new Nation. The second of the two cautioned that the light-skinned race might come wearing the face of death, but that it would look almost the same as the face of brotherhood. Their hearts would be filled with greed, and they would carry weapons. He implored them not to be too trusting, and that they would know that the face they wore is that of death if "the rivers run with poison and fish become unfit to eat."

The Fifth Prophet stated that in the time of the Fifth Fire there would be a great struggle between the natural path of the spirit of Native American Peoples and the way of life of the light-skinned people. He told them that some would falsely promise prosperity and salvation if they turned to the new ways but warned that if the old ways were abandoned, the struggle would continue for many generations.

The Sixth Prophet told them that during the Sixth Fire it would become crystal clear that the promise accepted during the Fifth Fire had been false. Those who were hoodwinked by it would take their children away from the teachings of the Elders, resulting in the Elders losing their purpose in life, becoming sick, and dying. It was to be a time of great imbalance, grief, and pain.

The Seventh Prophet was different than the previous prophets—he was younger and had a light about him. He told them that in the time of the Seventh Fire, a New People would emerge. It would be a time when nature was decaying, with animals and plants sick and dying. These New People would retrace their steps and find the treasures that had been left along the trail, and the stories that had been lost would be found once more. They would remember the Original Instructions, find strength in the old ways, and find the Elders, who they must carefully ask for guidance. If the New People are able to trust in their Traditional ways, they'll be able to find their inner voice, wisdom will return to their dreams, and the Sacred Fire will again be lit. This time, it will be the light-skinned people who will have to make one of two choices. If they choose the right road, the Seventh Fire will light the Eighth Fire, one of brotherhood and sisterhood that ushers in an era of peace and love. If they make the wrong choice, the destruction they initially brought will return and cause death and suffering to all.

The Chippewa believe all these prophecies have come to pass and that we are currently at a crossroads between materialism and technology and spirituality. This is a crucial time in human history, as we approach the fork in the road.

Prophecies are common across Native American Nations as well as in non-Native religions. What is most striking about the Seven Fires Prophecy is how seemingly accurate it was. It depicts the displacements that the Chippewa and many other Native American Nations experienced during the colonial period with alarming detail.
What prophecies are you familiar with?
Do they resonate with what you've learned about the history of your own culture?

DREAMS AND VISION QUESTS

The Chippewa believe that human beings have two souls: one that lives during waking moments of the day, and another that travels at night and lives the dream that the sleeping person is having. Thanks to this second soul, they can communicate with the Spirits and with the souls of nonhumans.

It is through dreams and visions that the Chippewa believe they gain powerful insight into their own needs, goals, and desires. Whole ceremonies are dedicated to acquiring the knowledge and meaning of dreams, including fasting or depriving oneself of certain essential items as a way to enhance one's ability to fully access their dreams and visions. These rituals often took place during certain specific points in the Chippewa People's lives. For instance, young adolescents would fast to provoke vivid dreams that might give them insight on their future choices and behaviors. It was a time of solitude that was integral to young people finding their purpose and direction. Sweat lodges were also a big part of the use of dreams as a means of healing.

While many of these dreams or vision quests happened individually, there were also annual fasts and community dream Ceremonies to renew the group's vision and reflect on their life cycles. Each community would have a Dreamer in place; this person was considered a visionary who had access to dreams of powerful consequence and considerable weight. Often these dreams were prophetic in nature and were used to predict imminent danger.

DREAM CATCHERS

As was mentioned in the introduction of this book, Dream Catchers are commonly appropriated by non-Natives. But far from being a design element for someone's eclectically decorated bedroom, Dream Catchers are items of great significance and value for the Chippewa.

According to the Chippewa, Dream Catchers are actually a way to trap the bad dreams that fly openly in the night air and keep them from entering the mind of the person they are protecting. They were meant to facilitate a child's ability to acquire good dreams and filter out the frightening, gloomy, or negative ones, and were considered just as effective for kids as they are for adults and families, often hung above a family's sleeping area to offer protection to the group as a whole. The concept of Dream Catchers eventually spread to the Lakota, who, over time, developed their own rituals and Traditions around them. However, it remains a common misconception that all or most Native American Nations use Dream Catchers. It is a belief rooted in Chippewa spirituality and is the result of a Dream Catcher Oral Tradition.

It is said that a grandmother patiently watched as a spider spun its web above her sleeping area. Her grandson spotted the spider and quickly moved to kill it. The grandmother surprised him by softly telling him not to kill it. He didn't understand why she would keep it alive, but eventually left it alone and headed to his own home. After the grandson left, the spider thanked the woman for protecting it, and offered her a gift in return. He spun her a web to hang between her and the moon, so that when she dreamed it would snare the bad thoughts and keep them from her, only allowing the good to pass through.

CHILDREN AND THE VISION QUEST

Children start fasting sometimes as young as five years old in an attempt to receive visions. Their faces and arms would be blackened with ash before being taken to the Place of Visions. This was usually somewhere that was removed from the daily happenings of the community, and was considered to be peculiar and oddly artificial—a place not constructed by either humans or nature. It was during these special occasions that the Spirits would welcome the human visitors. The parent would make an offering of tobacco and ask the Spirits to bring their child a vision, then they would depart, leaving the child alone for several days while awaiting this vision.

This vision would often come in the form of a specific animal who would give the child special instructions for their life, including teaching them special songs and showing them how to use special medicines. This animal would become this child's personal Manitou, or Spirit, and the person would carry a likeness to symbolize the essence of their spiritual power. The Chippewa believe that during Creation, each animal was given the ability to know the future as well as being given an additional special gift. Throughout the course of their lives, each person can call on their guardian Spirit for guidance, protection, and help to understand the future during difficult times. When a Spirit comes to a human during a dream or vision quest, they may choose to share their gift with the human. For example, plant Spirits were given the gift of healing, and it is believed that when people were visited by plants in their dreams, they often became healers.

The vision quest remains a way for Chippewa to seek out the wisdom of The Creator. It is a grueling process that requires profound physical sacrifice that is repaid by giving people spiritual power, songs that allow them to communicate with the Spirits, and medicines. When the vision quest is over, the person is expected to publicly share their experience through a Sacred song or dance that was taught to them by their Guardian Spirit, though paintings were also acceptable.

Over the centuries, the Chippewa developed various spiritual rituals that were used as part of Ceremonies, in their daily lives, or both. Dream Catchers, also known as Sacred Hoops, were precious talismans meant to protect sleeping people. They are used as everyday objects with powerful spiritual significance.

COMMON
CHIPPEWA RITUALS

An integral part of Chippewa culture and spirituality since Mythic Time, many of the following rituals are still performed today by the Chippewa and neighboring Nations. These rituals are good examples of Native American Traditions that have been appropriated to the point that they are mainstream. Most people don't even know their origins! As you read through them, are there any that jump out at you as rituals you are familiar with, have seen, or perhaps have participated in yourself?

SMUDGING

This purification rite usually involved using one of four Sacred Medicines: tobacco, sage, cedar, or sweetgrass. The smoke should envelop a person, place, thing, or situation as a means of cleansing and ushering in hope. As we highlighted previously, this is a practice that has been widely appropriated by non-Natives, to the point that certain varieties of sage are at risk of becoming endangered due to over-harvesting. If non-Natives are interested in performing their own ritual cleanse, it would be more appropriate to consider alternatives like salt sprays or incense.

SWEAT LODGES

The Chippewa connected with the Spirits while visiting a sweat lodge, a small construction with heated rocks that would induce profuse, deep sweating in the participant. Prayers and rituals during this event can provide healing and clarity.

POWWOWS

These Ceremonies were held for a wide variety of reasons and called for dancing, feasting, and rejoicing. They were used as a means of community bonding, naming children, and even supporting sobriety.

DRUM CIRCLES

During a drum circle, Chippewa People believe that the voice of the Spirit comes to the drummers and that they are able to impart that voice to the people through the drums.

SACRED PIPES

These carefully stored, prepared, and held pipes are used for prayer. The belief is that as the smoke rises, so do the prayers.

GIFT EXCHANGES

Exchanging gifts is a way for the community to connect with one another through giving.

MIDEWIWIN

The word *Midewiwin* refers to the Grand Medicine Lodge Society, a spiritual organization made up of both men and women who serve as spiritual advisors, leaders, and healers for the community. They are an essential component of Chippewa culture, performing Ceremonies, studying and practicing Sacred healing methods, and always working to maintain a harmonious relationship between humans and nature.

This group of people were initiated into the society through a variety of rites and steps during a Ceremony that conferred great power. Twice a year, in the late spring and early fall, the Midewiwin would hold these rites, and each celebration lasted several days. The Chippewa believe this Ceremony is necessary for healing, well-being, and to fend off evil Spirits so that they could instead follow a wholesome, righteous path. Purification in a sweat lodge was required before participation in the Ceremonies, and is one of the first rites to occur.

Depending on the community, there are four to eight tiers of Midewiwin membership. Each tier has its own initiation rites, periods of education, and methods of instruction. The higher an individual ascended in the organization, the more knowledge and healing power was bestowed upon them. In the past there was a financial cost to gain entry to each tier, though, for the most part, those have now been removed.

Colonizers originally referred to Midewiwin as a secret, closed society, though it's now known that this is not true, as it provided services to the community at large as needed. This misinformation was likely the result of an inability to understand the more nuanced details of Chippewa culture and spirituality, and because it is very likely that they simply were not invited to or welcome at Midewiwin Ceremonies. Today, the Midewiwin primarily participate in the reciting of Sacred Stories and songs, the practice of herbal remedies, and performing dances through which they receive their powers to heal and cure. It is a resilient institution that has survived centuries of religious and cultural persecution.

DEVELOPING
YOUR OWN RITUAL

In any society, a ritual can mean many things. In Western culture, this can mean anything from a morning routine to the celebration of holidays. Different forms of Christianity are rife with rituals. For example, in Catholicism, baptism is a ritual that is said to cleanse a baby of original sin, which they are born into. The taking of the Eucharist symbolizes the sacrifice made by Jesus when he died for the sins of humanity. In Wicca, a ritual is typically a set practice that serves a purpose, like calling on the help of a deity, performing a spell, or performing a meditation. But there are other, more casual rituals that people perform daily, like having a morning cup of coffee, adopting an exercise routine, or even having meals in community.

Consider your own rituals and think about the following prompts.

> ≫ What rituals do you perform to mark holidays?
> ≫ What rituals do you perform to start and end your day?
> ≫ If you were to change geographical locations, would your rituals change?
> ≫ Now choose one of your values and think of a way that you can create a ritual to honor that value.

CHAPTER 8

THE SEVEN SACRED RITES OF THE SIOUX NATION

The Great Sioux Nation is a confederation of seven different Nations known as the Oceti Sakowin, meaning "Seven Council Fires." These Nations speak three dialects of the same language family: Dakota, Nakota, and Lakota, which became known as the Sioux in the seventeenth century. Dakota speakers are called the Isantis (or sometimes Santees). They make up four Council Fires: the Mdewakantunwan, Sisitunwan, Wahpetunwan, and Wahpekute. The Nakota speakers are known as the Wiciyelas and include two Council Fires: the Yanktons and Yanktonai. The Lakota speakers, Titunwans, make up the single Western Council Fire, which includes the Oglala, Sicangu, Hunkpapa, Minneconjou, Itzipco, Oohenunpa, and Sihasapa.

CREATION AND SPIRITUALITY

The Lakota reside in what is now known as both North and South Dakota, while the Dakota live primarily in Minnesota and Nebraska. The Nakota, the smallest of the three Tribes, reside in South Dakota, North Dakota, and Montana. Since time immemorial they have lived in areas stretching across the Great Plains, and many of their belief systems, values, and rituals directly correlate to the importance of a successful bison-hunting season. The Lakota People are even more deeply rooted in the Great Plains, as their Creation Oral Tradition states that they emerged from a cave in the Black Hills of South Dakota. It's a deeply Sacred place for them, where The Creator bestowed on them the Sacred Pipe and the Seven Sacred Rites, including the Sun Dance, during a visit from the White Buffalo Calf Woman.

They believe that they, along with the bison, emerged from Wind Cave in the Southern Black Hills. Wind Cave is one of the longest and most complex cave systems in the world, with the first of these presently designated as a National Park. It has a unique boxwork formation, which makes the walls of the caves look like honeycombs made of thin calcite slabs.

The Lakota believe that before their time on Earth, they lived within these caves, below the surface in what they called Tunkan Tipi, the Spirit Lodge. It was a time when The Creator was still working hard to bring plants and animals into existence on the surface of the Earth, but it was not yet ready for humans. The Creator asked them to remain in Wind Cave while preparations finished, but two Spirits who lived on the surface, Iktomi and Anog-Ite, had other plans. Iktomi was the spider trickster Spirit and Anog-Ite was the double-faced woman Spirit—one of the two faces on her head was beautiful, while the other was twisted, frightening, and terrible. Iktomi and Anog-Ite were both outcasts who lived a lonely existence, with only each other for company. Iktomi was forever playing tricks on and antagonizing Anog-Ite, but even that eventually became boring. So he convinced Anog-Ite to help him play a trick on the humans, promising her he'd never torment her again if she did so.

Anog-Ite filled a pack with intricate buckskin clothing, berries, and dried meat, then tied it to the back of her wolf companion. Iktomi led the wolf to the hole in the ground that marked the passageway to the Spirit Lodge and sent him to find the humans who were waiting there. Once there, he told the people about the beauty and magic of the Earth's surface. The wolf told them to come out to the surface and he'd show them how to acquire these delicacies for themselves. One human refused to go, saying that he wouldn't betray The Creator's trust. Most of the people agreed and stayed back with him, but all those who had tried the meat followed the wolf to the surface. It was a beautiful summer day, and they were awed by the wondrous nature. The wolf led them to Anog-Ite, who had covered her horrible face so that only her beautiful one could be seen. She taught the people how to hunt, work, and tan animal hides. The people, who had very easy lives in the Spirit Lodge, had never had to work so hard before, and when the seasons changed and winter came, they began to freeze and starve. They returned to Anog-Ite, begging for help, but she revealed her frightening, ugly face and laughed. The humans ran back to the hole in terror, only to find that it had been covered and they were trapped on the surface.

The Creator heard them despairing and asked them how they came to be on the surface. They explained what had happened, but he was displeased with them. He punished them by transforming them into great wild beasts—the first bison herd. Once time passed and the Earth was finally ready, The Creator instructed the people who had remained within the cave to make their way through the passageway to the surface. They stopped to pray four times along the way, stopping last at the entrance. Once there, they saw a bison's footprints. The Creator instructed them to follow the bison, for that would be how they acquired food, tools, clothes, and shelter, and lead them to water. Everything they needed to survive on the Earth could come from the bison. After the people left the cave, The Creator shrunk the hole to the size it is now—too small for people to enter, but visible and accessible, so that the Lakota would never forget where they'd come from.

The Titunwans, while only representing a single unified Council Fire, are made up of seven sub-Bands, each with their own unique set of Traditions and values largely influenced by their geographical location and surroundings. This is reflected in the meaning of their names.

OGLALA—Scatter One's Own
SICANGU—Burnt Thigh
HUNKPAPA—Those Who Camp at the Entrance
MINNECONJOU—Those Who Plant by the Stream
ITZIPCO—Without Bows
OOHENUNPA—Two Kettles
SIHASAPA—Black Feet

THE SACRED BUNDLE

The Lakota believe that the Sacred White Buffalo Calf Woman came to them and gave them a Sacred Bundle containing the Sacred Pipe and a small round stone—gifts to be used during the first of seven rites that would be revealed to them.

The Sacred Pipe

The Sacred Pipe is a key component of Lakota spirituality and culture. They believe the smoke rises up to connect them to the Spirits. As they exhale, it carries offering of prayers and thoughts upwards. The Lakota take their commitment to the pipe very seriously; it can only be used for good purposes to bring harmony between people. Each part of the pipe is a representation of their relationship with different parts of the world.

> » The stem of the pipe is wood, representing the plants and all that grows on Earth.
>
> » The bowl is made of red stone to symbolize the Earth and features a carving of a buffalo head, representing four-legged animals.
>
> » Tobacco represents humans.
>
> » The breath symbolizes the elements.
>
> » Twelve eagle feathers hang from the notch where the bowl meets the stem, symbolizing all birds.

After the gifts were used for the first rite, the Sacred White Buffalo Calf Woman changed from a beautiful young woman to a black buffalo, then a red-brown buffalo, then a yellow buffalo, and finally into a white buffalo. Then she disappeared into the clouds. It is believed that the Sacred Bundle that the Sacred White Buffalo Calf Woman gave the Lakota still exists to this day and has been passed down through nineteen generations. Chief Avril Looking Horse is the current Keeper of the Sacred Pipe and Spiritual Leader for the Sioux Nation. The responsibility was passed to him by his grandmother at the age of twelve.

THE SEVEN RITES

In order to preserve their culture, Traditions, and continued survival, the Lakota perform the Seven Rites. Each has its own individual powers and purpose, and acts as a means to remain connected with The Creator. They are integral components of the Lakota's spiritual life.

THE FIRST RITE: KEEPING OF THE SOUL

The Lakota believe that when a person dies, their soul has to be purified in order to reunite with The Creator. A lock of hair is taken from the deceased and held over burning sweetgrass to purify it. Then it is wrapped into what is known as the soul bundle, a sacred buckskin bundle that is placed in the Keeper of the Soul's tipi. The Keeper of the Soul would then vow to live a life of harmony for about a year, until the soul could be released.

To release the soul, the Ceremony begins with a buffalo hunt and the building of a special lodge. Sacred tobacco is smoked, and an offering is made to the Earth by burying special food. The Sacred bundle holding the hair is carried outside and the soul is released as soon as it touches the outdoor air. It is believed the soul travels along the Spirit Path, which non-Natives know as the Milky Way, until it reaches Maya Owichapaha, an old woman who judges each soul. If it is deemed worthy, she sends the soul straight to The Creator. If it is deemed unworthy, they remain until they can become purified, then they join The Creator.

THE SECOND RITE:
INIPI, THE RITE OF PURIFICATION

Inipi—translated to mean "to live again"—is the Lakota word for a sweat lodge (see page 116). This is a purification rite that is necessary for anyone on a vision quest in order to experience a spiritual rebirth, and is done before major life or seasonal events to purify the body while also gaining strength and power. The lodge itself is a dome made of sixteen young willow trees placed in a circle and sealed with hides. There is a mound of earth just outside the door, facing east, and a fire pit filled with stones that represents the sun. Another mound of dirt partially encircles the fire pit and represents the crescent moon. The inner world of the sweat lodge represents the womb of the universe, which can make souls new.

The prayers that are offered up during the Inipi draw on all the powers of Earth, Water, Fire, and Air. They are said at every stage of the sweat lodge's construction. After it's ready, the Lakota bring in burning coal and sweetgrass, which is burned by the Spiritual Leader to purify the lodge. The Pipe is smoked, carried outside, and placed on a mound of earth. Once the other participants enter the lodge, they are seated in a circle on Sacred sage, after which the Pipe is brought back inside and smoked. The heated rocks are placed on the fireplace and the door is closed. Throughout the ceremony, the door is opened four times, representing the four ages described by the Sacred White Buffalo Calf Woman. (When she first came to them, she explained that there would be four ages of time, and that she would look in on them at each age.) The fourth time it is opened, the participants leave the lodge. Their emergence from the dark into the light is representative of an unshackling from the physical realm, and all impurities are left in the sweat lodge.

THE THIRD RITE: CRYING FOR A VISION

Anyone wishing to go on a Vision Quest undergoes the Crying for a Vision rite in an effort to pray, liaise with Spirits, and obtain knowledge, wisdom, and strength. With the help and guidance of a holy Spiritual Leader who can interpret the Vision, the person remains isolated on a hill for up to four days with just a blanket and a pipe, foregoing food and water the entire time. And while any man or woman can "cry for a vision," not everyone receives one.

A person undertaking a Vision Quest must first go to the Spiritual Leader, asking him to be their guide and to pray for them. Anyone who is present smokes the Pipe, after which they conduct the Inipi Ceremony for purification. In this instance, the seeker builds the sweat lodge by himself, without the assistance of anyone else. He then takes his pipe and tobacco and goes to the designated place of isolation, generally a bluff or high mountain. He or she stays at this location and prays for a Vision. When these Visions arrive, they often come in the form of an animal, usually in dreams, which are considered to carry the most powerful Visions. At the end of the Vision Quest, the seeker returns to the sweat lodge, usually with the help of others. He then tells the Spiritual Leader everything he's seen and heard so that its meaning can be interpreted.

THE FOURTH RITE: THE SUN DANCE

The Sun Dance is revered as the most significant of the Seven Sacred Rites. It is a twelve-day Ceremony that took place in the summer and emphasized self-sacrifice, courage, and endurance, all in the name of serving The Creator. As it was the most important Ceremony practiced by the Sioux, it was considered a time of immense renewal. Everything was done to please the Spirits in the hope that they would bring lots of bison. Many Bands would come together for this annual rite, each camped within their own circle. The Ceremony would take place in the Sun Dance Lodge to create a space for prayer, sacrifice, dancing, and healing. It was a temporary structure built out of saplings and brush, with a pole in the middle made from a Sacred cottonwood tree, which Spiritual Leaders would select from the forest.

Before the commencement of the Sun Dance, everyone participating was purified through the Inipi. Each dancer would have a mentor of sorts, usually a Spiritual Leader or someone who had done the dance in years prior, to help him get through the Ceremony. The Ceremony would begin at sunrise, and everyone was invited to dance. Dancers would look at the sun while they danced, and short breaks were allowed, albeit without food or water. Over the course of three or four days, dancers move from the circular edge of the lodge to the tree at the center and back again, always facing and placing their concentration on the center pole and the sun. It was rare for women to participate, and the men who did were usually asking for specific wishes to be granted, such as better hunting and fighting skills, or even healing powers. They wore sage rings on their heads, wrists, and ankles, and carried whistles made from an eagle's wing bone.

While the dancing happened, the Spiritual Leaders would pierce the dancers' bodies with pieces of animal bones, attaching some of them to the pole, while others were attached to buffalo skulls that they dragged behind themselves. The purpose of the dance was to remove the attached pieces of bone from their bodies. If they hadn't been successful in removing them by sundown, either mentors or the Spiritual Leaders would remove them. Unsurprisingly, this was a traumatic experience for many dancers. Afterwards, they would go to the dancers' lodge to be cared for by medicine men and Spiritual Leaders who would pray for them and sing their praises to The Creator.

The Sun Dance was criminalized in the United States in 1883 by the Secretary of the Interior and the Bureau of Indian Affairs, along with other Sacred Ceremonies. This was done to discourage Native practices as part of a larger effort by the government to force assimilation and undermine Native cultures, and it did a lot of long-term damage. For fifty years, the Sun Dance remained illegal, until 1934 when President Roosevelt reversed the decision. During that time, the Lakota defied the ban by continuing to perform this most sacred dance in secret, often as part of Fourth of July celebrations. Sun Dances are performed to this day every year, though due to the importance of the Ceremony, only Native people are allowed to participate. It is forbidden to film any part of the Ceremony or prayers, and there are many who still believe that if money or cameras set foot in the Dance circle, the Spirits leave.

In response to what they felt was the disrespect and desecration of Sacred Ceremonies, American and Canadian Lakota, Dakota, and Nakota Nations held the Lakota Summit V in 1993. Five hundred representatives from forty different Nations passed a "Declaration of War Against Exploiters of Lakota Spirituality" without opposition. It prohibits non-Native people from participating in Sacred Ceremonies as well as outlawing the exploitation, abuse, and misrepresentation of said Ceremonies. In 2003, the current Keeper of the Sacred White Buffalo Calf Pipe asked non-Native people to stop attending the Sun Dance altogether. He had the support of other Keepers of Sacred Bundles and Traditional Spiritual Leaders from the Cheyenne, Dakota, and Nakota Nations, who issued a proclamation that non-Natives would be banned from Sacred altars and all of the Seven Sacred Rites, including, and especially, the Sun Dance.

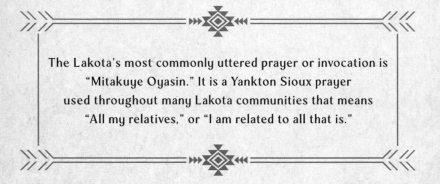

The Lakota's most commonly uttered prayer or invocation is "Mitakuye Oyasin." It is a Yankton Sioux prayer used throughout many Lakota communities that means "All my relatives," or "I am related to all that is."

THE FIFTH RITE:
THE MAKING OF RELATIVES

First used to make peace between Nations in conflict, the Making of Relatives Ceremony (also known as the Hunka or Hunkapi) was about separate families coming together and joining as one to become treasured relatives. The Lakota believe that it mirrors the relationship between them and The Creator. The object of this Ceremony is to bind two people, or sometimes entire families, to each other, creating a special kind of unique kinship. These ties of fidelity are considered the strongest that one can have, and the intensity of that bond can best be likened to that of parent and child. It is considered a peace Ceremony, and once two people have been joined, they are considered reborn and responsible for their new relationships, and past issues are forgotten.

When it comes to relatives of any kind, including Hunka-bound family members, Lakota kinship terms differ between men and women. What a girl would call her parents or grandparents differs from what a boy might call them. Women would call their mothers "At'e," and their fathers "Musunkala," while a younger brother would be "Mitankala" and a younger sister "Cuwe." Men would call their mothers "Ina," their fathers "At'e," their younger brothers "Misunkala," and younger sisters "Mitankala." There is a nuanced complexity to these names that adds meaning and affection.

THE SIXTH RITE:
A GIRL'S COMING OF AGE

A Girl's Coming of Age Ceremony is considered to be preparation for the start of their sacred journey to womanhood and is performed upon the arrival of a girl's first menstruation. Traditionally, her family would build a sweat lodge and gather the necessary objects for Purification Rites. On the day of the Ceremony, sweetgrass would be burned, and Ceremonial objects would be cleansed with the smoke. Prayers were offered up to The Creator, the four directions, and the Earth. The girl would then be isolated from the rest of the community and begin a four-day Ceremony that was taught to her by other women.

During this time, the girls cannot touch food or drink and are instead fed by their mothers and other women who are participating. The girls are taught the roles and responsibilities that they will assume as women in their communities, including quill work. After four days, they are presented to their communities as women. Songs are sung and the girls eat and thank the people who have helped them. This rite is still performed, though now it is a symbolic camp that is set up once a year that is attended by preteen and young teen girls for four days.

THE SEVENTH RITE: THE THROWING OF THE BALL

Though the Throwing of the Ball may outwardly appear to be a sports game, it is infused with meaning and devotion to The Creator at all times. Traditionally, the ball was made of buffalo hair and covered with buffalo hide. In a Ceremony that takes place before the throwing, the ball would be made Sacred by being painted red with a blue dot in each of the four quarters. Two blue circles were then painted around the circumference of the ball to represent the joining of the cosmos and the Earth. A pipe filled with sweetgrass was used to purify the event, sending smoke up to The Creator and the four directions. Since the ball had been given to the people by the buffalo, it symbolized that man inherited the Earth.

A young girl, symbolizing innocence and purity, was chosen to throw the ball. She stood at the center of a circle, first throwing the ball to the west, then to the three other directions. Finally, she would throw the ball up in the air. The throwing of the ball noted The Creator's presence everywhere, and as the ball comes back down, His power also comes down, though few may receive or catch it.

THE TERMS WE USE

Although terms of endearment might differ among families or communities, there are also common regional words and descriptors for our loved ones. What family nicknames do you have for your immediate loved ones? Does anyone outside your home use those names, or are they special and private?

Interview three friends from different backgrounds. Ask them what they call their family members, both in private and in public. Are there any commonalities? What stands out to you about the differences? Are they the result of different languages, backgrounds, or ethnicities? Are they pet names that have evolved over time?

The words we use to call out for those we care for are held precious and help form a deeper, more personal bond.

CHAPTER 9

THE THREE BASIC LAWS OF THE CHUMASH NATION

The Chumash were the first human inhabitants of the California coast, from Malibu to Paso Robles, including the Channel Islands, the Santa Monica Mountains, and even stretching slightly inland to the western edge of the San Joaquin Valley. Prior to the Mission Period, the Chumash lived in more than 150 independent villages and spoke six different, but related, languages. The Chumash are a maritime culture, and because different villages along the coast and on the islands had access to different resources, they would trade with each other via plank canoes. As a result, there is no single homogenous Chumash culture (which can generally be said is the case for most large Native American Nations), with a wide range of diverse beliefs among the various communities.

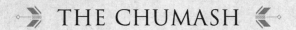

THE CHUMASH

The Chumash call themselves The First People, and consider the Pacific Ocean their first home. These hunters, gatherers, and fishermen lived in large dome-shaped houses made of willow branches, and used the natural resources around them to make boats, baskets, and stone cookware. Depending on which part of the region they lived in, the Chumash ranged from laborers to skilled crafters, Chiefs, Spiritual Leaders called Shamans, and astronomers. In Chumash culture, women could serve equally, both as Chiefs and as Shamans. They would find and use caves for their Sacred religious ceremonies, most of which still exist today but are protected by the National Parks system. These caves and the art they contain emphasize the spiritual bond between the Chumash and their natural environment.

THE TOMOLS

The plank canoes, which the Chumash call tomols, were usually made from redwood or pine logs. As a result of their maritime culture and a rich trading economy, Chumash People have never been dependent upon agriculture, just like many other Native American Nations. They lived on acorns, seeds, nuts, and roots as well as wild game such as bears, seals, otters, shellfish, deer, and whales. They have always been and still are extremely resourceful and innovative, finding multiple uses for plants and bones to create woven baskets, tools, and clothing.

CUSTOMS AND BELIEFS

As with so many Native American Nations, there are similarities in their cultures, beliefs, and way of life. But the Chumash are unique in their invention and use of the plank canoe, their stunning basketry techniques, use and creation of tools, and bead making. It is their customs and beliefs, as well as their craftsmanship, that make the Chumash incredibly unique. Ceremonial Dances were often held to honor the many creatures in the Chumash Nation's natural environment. People would come from neighboring towns to celebrate the Bear, Blackbird, Fox, and Coyote. The most important Ceremonial Dance held by the Chumash was the Swordfish Dance, which we'll take a closer look at later in the chapter.

HARMONY

Living in harmony with nature and creating a sustainable existence is paramount to Chumash culture. They believe that man's natural greedy nature and need to control everything—from other people to the land—gets in the way of and disrupts the natural order of things. It is through Sacred Fires, Ceremonies, and Dances that they remember the Traditional ways that can never truly be taken from them. Prayers and Ceremonies enable them to listen to their ancestors and learn their ways, reminding them to respect the balance of nature.

THE THREE BASIC LAWS OF THE CHUMASH

The Chumash have always been aware of and observed the effect they have on the land and wilderness. Nature taught the Chumash about the balance between the physical, the spiritual, and the natural world, and they witnessed firsthand the consequences of disrespecting their environment. As a result, the Chumash live by three basic laws that they believe establish harmony and balance in the world. They apply these three laws mentally, physically, and spiritually, and live by them on a daily basis.

- » **LIMITATION**—Once one identifies and accepts their limitations as human beings who are going to live and die, one can better and more easily accept who they are as individuals. A person can only do so much.

- » **MODERATION**—This applies both to what is taken from the land and their approach to work. Only take what you need from the land and oceans; leave the rest for another day and for others. Don't try to do everything at once; leave some work for tomorrow.

- » **COMPENSATION**—True compensation comes in many forms, whether it be happiness, health, wealth, or even the arrival of a beloved child. If you want to do something generous or kind for someone else or for the land, do it out of the goodness of your heart and not because you expect something in return. The Chumash believe that it comes when you need it most and least expect it.

THE SWORDFISH DANCE AND CAVE

Swordfish feature prominently in Chumash culture, particularly in the Santa Barbara region, and was considered the Chief of all sea animals—in essence, the marine equivalent to humans on land. In fact, the Chumash believed that there were a direct underwater equivalent to every living being on land. They considered sardines the lizards of the ocean, while lobsters were the crickets of the sea. The Chumash believed that when whales became beached, or stranded on the shore, it was the result of being chased ashore by the swordfish. Whales provided an abundance of food for the Chumash, making swordfish especially venerated. This didn't stop the Chumash from consuming the swordfish, but they were seen as being incredibly powerful creatures.

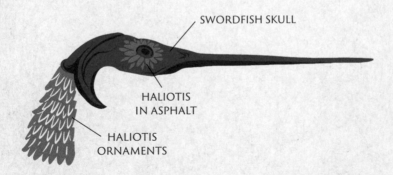

SWORDFISH SKULL

HALIOTIS
IN ASPHALT

HALIOTIS
ORNAMENTS

The regalia of the Swordfish Dancer was incredibly ornate. Most commonly, the dancer would often wear an actual swordfish skull that was decorated with an intricate shell inlay, though at times headdresses were worn that symbolized the fish's sword via the use of feathers instead of a sword. During the Ceremony, the dancer would twirl in a circle, sometimes so quickly that the sword on the headdress looked like a spinning wheel. He would spin in one direction, then another, always giving thanks to The Creator. Throughout the Ceremony, Sacred offerings would be made of beads and other gifts. Upon their deaths, Swordfish Dancers would be buried with their headdresses.

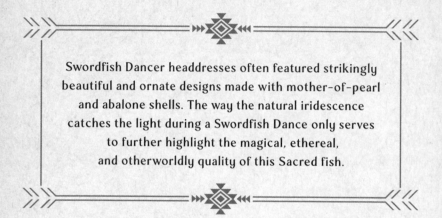

Swordfish Dancer headdresses often featured strikingly beautiful and ornate designs made with mother-of-pearl and abalone shells. The way the natural iridescence catches the light during a Swordfish Dance only serves to further highlight the magical, ethereal, and otherworldly quality of this Sacred fish.

CHUMASH ROCK ART

Swordfish also feature prominently in Chumash rock art sites. Its prominence in both the Swordfish Dance and the Nation's artwork is indicative of what a significant role this fish has played in the culture's rituals and spiritual beliefs. Chumash Shamans made elaborate and colorful rock art that represented spiritual figures from their Oral Traditions, natural marvels, or abstract notions. Red, white, and black are the most common colors used in these cave paintings. Red ink was made from hematite, white from gypsum, and black from charcoal or manganese oxide. The pigments would be ground into a powder, then mixed with a binding agent like plant juices, water, or even animal fat to turn them into paint. The Chumash would then use their fingers or brushes made from animal tails to make their renderings. In some locations, chalk-like lines made with dry lumps of pigment can be found.

Swordfish Cave

Used as a campsite while hunting and gathering, Swordfish Cave in Santa Barbara County remains a Sacred location to this day and is considered the point through which the departed pass on the way to the afterlife. Early inhabitants laid down a bedrock mortar in the cave floor to be used for grinding plant foods, and it is still readily visible. It is bursting with petroglyphs and pictographs depicting swordfish as well as people and other animals. Rock paintings remain Sacred to the Chumash, and because they are incredibly fragile, preserving them is of the utmost importance. Because they can be so easily damaged, the majority of rock art locations are not open or even known to non-Native people, with the exception of Painted Cave State Historic Park, near Santa Barbara.

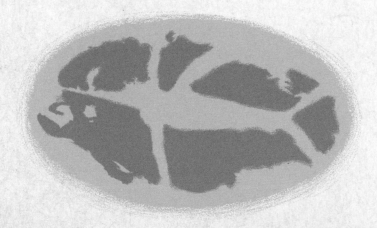

An example of a rock painting from Swordfish Cave.

TIME, THE SEASONS, AND THE CIRCLE OF LIFE

Like other Native Americans highly attuned to nature and the land, the Chumash lived in accordance with the seasons. They believed that, just like the salmon who knew when to swim upstream and the birds who knew when to fly south or north for the winter, surrendering to and becoming a part of nature was the only way to understand the passage of time. Presently, they believe that if we stop living by the time of man and instead embrace the cyclical time of nature, people will find enlightenment.

The Chumash consider themselves to be responsible for their land and the natural world. By paying close attention to the seasons, the way the land changes, and the sounds of the living beings, they can find insight into how to maintain the balance between them and their surroundings. These are lessons that teach them respect for medicinal plants, how to make their homes, and sustainability—all of which contribute to their continued survival. They believe that land, water, and air are the three bodies of life that sustain them and on which their existence is completely dependent.

Each of the four seasons is believed to be represented by each of the cardinal directions, certain animals, and even specific emotions. Winter is considered the north and the color white, which represents the winter solstice. The eagle and bear are the animal symbols of the winter season. The eagle represents human beings' pride and strength, and the bear represents the strength of Mother Earth. The Chumash do not believe one animal is stronger than the other; instead, they work in harmony to protect each other and the land. Summer is the south and the color blue, which is reflected in the region's warm winds and gently lulling ocean waves. The animal representatives of the summer season are the owl and the snake; the owl represents wisdom, and encouraging a sharp mind, while the snake represents the sensitive side of Mother Earth. The Chumash believe that as a snake glides over the Earth he can feel her passionate emotions like waves rippling across the surface of the sea.

Spring is the east and the color yellow, symbolic of the arrival of the sun and new life. The hawk and deer are the animal representatives of the spring season; the deer symbolizes life, and the hawk is its helper. The arrival of spring is widely celebrated with Oral Traditions, songs, and dances held in honor of the season. Fall is the west, and red represents the colors of the sky during a sunset. It is considered a transitional time, and also the time of the dolphin and its helper, the raven. They watch the spirits leave this world as the sun sets and the Milky Way appears.

The Chumash have Ceremonies that honor many of the cyclical events in the natural world, from the changing of the seasons to the return of a highly valued plant or animal. It is always a call for people to surrender themselves to the larger powers that control seasonal changes.

CHUMASH CHILDREN

Another important way to ensure future harmony is by exposing children to nature and teaching them about their responsibility to the larger world around them. With so many available life paths to choose from, it's important that children chart the right course, without influence from outside beliefs that are harmful to the future of Chumash culture, wildlife, and the planet.

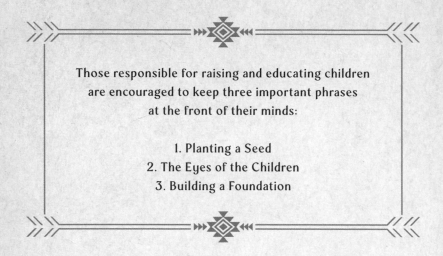

Those responsible for raising and educating children
are encouraged to keep three important phrases
at the front of their minds:

1. Planting a Seed
2. The Eyes of the Children
3. Building a Foundation

The Chumash believe that it is important to plant a seed in a child's mind that will help nurture their strength, giving them a clearer understanding of how their choices can affect the future. They say that children's eyes do not lie, making it important to remain vigilant and pay attention to what they can learn from them. Building a foundation for a new world is the only way to ensure the survival of the culture. Making good choices that reinforce the Chumash way of life and language while keeping the practice of customs and Traditions alive is the only way to secure a long-lasting legacy.

THE RAINBOW BRIDGE

A significant tenet of Chumash spirituality is the Oral Tradition of the Rainbow Bridge, which they call Wishtoyo, that has its roots in their Creation story. Mother Earth, Hutash, buried the seeds of a magical plant on Santa Cruz Island, from which men and women sprung, fully formed. Mother Earth's husband, Sky Snake (known to non-Natives now as the Milky Way), gave them the gift of fire, so the people could cook food and stay warm. Thanks to the ability to make hot food, the Chumash were prosperous, happy, and fulfilled. But after many years the island became too crowded. They were depleting the island's fragile resources, and the noise of the Chumash singing, dancing, and laughing kept Hutash awake at night.

So she created a Rainbow Bridge for the Chumash People on Santa Cruz Island to cross over to the mainland, where there would be an abundance of food, land, and resources for their families. They started their journey across the bridge, and while most got across safely, some made the mistake of looking down. The bridge was very high up, and it was a long way down to the water, with fog swirling around them. They became dizzy and disoriented and fell off the rainbow bridge, down through the fog and into the ocean. Having been the one to tell them to cross the bridge, Hutash felt responsible for their deaths; she hadn't wanted them to drown. In order to save them, she turned them into dolphins.

For this reason, the Chumash see their connection to the ocean and the animals who live in it as not only spiritual, but familial as well, and they believe this accounts for the special bond that dolphins seem to have with humans. When men would go to sea on their fishing or trading expeditions, it was said that hundreds of dolphins would accompany them, and that when women gave birth on the shorelines, the dolphins would come and surround them, offering their protection. To this day, the Chumash call the dolphins their brothers and sisters.

It would be egregious to leave out the long-term ramifications that arose as a result of the California Mission System and its impact on the Chumash Nation. To better understand how the Chumash People's culture, beliefs, and practices were impacted, it's important to understand this particular version of forced assimilation that took place. While colonization occurred across the entire continent, the Mission System was unique to California and was responsible for complete and utter decimation of the Chumash way of life. The Chumash suffered years of declining population and had a very high infant mortality rate as a result of European-introduced diseases.

In 1769, Gaspar de Portola led a Spanish land expedition from Baja California to the Santa Barbara Channel. Within a very short period of time, five Spanish missions were established in Chumash territory, with the end goal being evangelization of all Native People in the area. In reality, it was systemic oppression, plain and simple, that was tantamount to slavery and genocide. Forced hard labor, deadly disease outbreaks, and prohibition of Native languages were the reality for the Chumash forced to live there. They were horribly mistreated under the Catholic Church, specifically the Franciscans who ran the Missions, even after the Mexican and Spanish governments had made attempts to put protections in place for Native Americans in California, promising them equal treatment under the law.

All this led to the Chumash Revolt of 1824, an organized rebellion that had been planned for months in advance. Despite this, the rebellion actually started a day early, when a young Chumash boy was badly beaten by a soldier while visiting a family member who was imprisoned at Mission Santa Inés. The Chumash, who were at the Mission, began the revolt early, burning down most of the Mission and attacking soldiers with arrows. They went on to execute coordinated attacks on Mission La Purisíma and Mission Santa Barbara. To the Chumash, this was a fight not just for their physical survival, but for their intellectual and spiritual survival as well. In fact, when soldiers went to find the Chumash who had fled to the hills after the rebellion, they were stunned to see that they had returned to their Traditional practices. The rebellion lasted nearly a month, and within five months, the majority of the Chumash who had fled the Missions had been returned to them.

The revolt didn't do much to change the outcome for the Chumash People, but it was the beginning of the end for the Mission System as a whole. Despite this, as a result of this forced assimilation and colonization, the Chumash language and culture was all but lost until very recently. The remaining survivors have worked hard over the last century to gain historical recognition and teach younger generations about their culture and their true history. There is still, however, much to be done to give the Chumash their rightful place in Californian culture and history.

MAKING A DIFFERENCE

The Native American Tribes covered in this book all have one important thing in common: their reverence for the land and their care of the environment. Consider the following suggestions for ways that you can lighten your own negative footprint on the environment in which you live. What are some additional ways in your own daily life that you can respect, revere, and care for the environment?

> » Stop buying single-use plastics. Take a canvas bag to the grocery store, adopt a favorite reusable water bottle, or refill cleaning products rather than buying new each time.

> » Purchase only what you need. Take stock of what you have and what you need. Often, we are targeted by ads telling us that we need particular items to make our lives easier. They can be convincing, but if you really think about it, do you really need it?

> » Give new life to what you already have. Repurpose common household items. Left with a large empty pickle jar? You can clean that and fill it with sugar that you use for baking with the added benefit of protecting it from pests. No longer love that dress? Cut it into cleaning rags that have a pattern and look that you love.

> » Do the simple things. Turn off lights as you leave the room, or turn the shower off while you soap up, only turning it on to rinse.

» Try composting. Composting reduces waste in landfills, while feeding and nourishing your garden.

» Go paperless with all of your bills.

» Declutter your home and donate what you don't need. This is one more way you can apply the "recycle/ reuse" philosophy.

» Walk or bike wherever you can. Cars have a huge carbon footprint.

» Use long-lasting light bulbs.

» Try meditating under a tree to connect with its energy.

In what other ways can you change your daily routines to have a more positive impact on the environment?

CHAPTER 10

MOVING FORWARD

Now that you have a richer and fuller understanding of the various nuances of Native American spiritual beliefs, practices, and culture, you can ruminate on the many things that they have to teach non-Natives. Use it as a jumping-off point for studying your own personal relationship with the world. Without appropriating Native American practices or spirituality, observe the effects of widening your understanding of this topic. See if it can help you view the world you live in a little differently, with a reverence towards nature, those around you, and a thoughtfulness as to the many ways, big and small, that we impact the environment we inhabit.

Having an accurate understanding of how our national history has shaped, influenced, and negatively affected Native American ways of life is the only way to really honor the Native experience and authentically learn about their cultures. Without that added layer of colonialism, forced assimilation, forced relocation, and evangelization, one simply cannot paint a full, complete picture of the Native American experience—from their daily routines to their most Sacred Oral Traditions and spiritual practices—both past and present. Facing these hard truths not only puts non-Natives in a position to hold people accountable, but it also lays the foundation for a lifetime of allyship. Now that you know how deeply held and rooted Native American practices are, you should feel empowered to call out appropriation as it happens. Anytime we take the opportunity to learn about people who have lived different experiences than our own, we open ourselves up to a greater understanding of ourselves, just as much as we do of the world around us.

By using this book as a resource to dispel previous misconceptions, broaden your own horizons, and enrich your perspectives, you can honor the legacy of Native Americans without further harming them. Try the various exercises throughout this book as a means to further understand the concepts presented herein, without adding to the trauma and defilement that has taken place for so long through ignorance and appropriation—both of which are long-standing side effects of colonialism.

A VARIETY OF
CULTURAL LESSONS

Each of the Native American Nations in this book have distinct beliefs and practices that are wholly unique to them, while also sharing pan-Indigenous commonalities. But that's never an excuse to lump them all into one group. Their distinctive defining characteristics are what make Native American culture so incredibly remarkable.

The Lenape's Oral Traditions bind them to the land on which they live. They teach them how to use the natural resources that are unique to that region and tie their Traditional Knowledge to their spiritual lives. It is the wellspring of their faith that all physical, spiritual, and cosmic elements are connected. The Seven Wise Men Oral Tradition is the ideal representation of this never-ending dynamic between the Lenape, nature, their spirituality, and the cosmos.

The Haudenosaunee's Seventh Generation value is something everyone can and should put into practice. The idea that we do not own the world we live in, rather, that we are borrowing it from future generations, only serves to foster a gentler, more thoughtful relationship with the environment around us. Let it influence your daily choices. Maybe it inspires you to reduce waste consumption in your daily life or motivates you to volunteer with at-risk youth organizations in your community. It could even be as simple as planting a garden in your neighborhood that everyone can enjoy while they're on their daily walks.

The Navajo Nation's art is wholly unique to their culture. Sandpainting and weaving, while art and craft forms on the surface, are filled with deeper symbolism, meaning, and power. It doesn't matter how practical the rug or blanket that a Navajo weaver might make may be, the act of making it is a spiritual process that was given to them by The Creator and is therefore endowed with their own unique energy. How do your own unique skills enhance your relationship with others around you?

The Cherokee Nation's resilience in the face of so many horrors informs so much of how they interact with the world, each other, and their spiritual practices. Stomp Dances remain opportunities for communities to strengthen their ties to each other through joyful dancing, feasting, and worship. These enthusiastic celebrations of thanksgiving and unity are key to the ensured survival of their culture.

The Chinook's Salmon Feast directly correlates to their natural environment and geographical location. It's the perfect example of how the unique features of their ancestral land influence every aspect of their spiritual life. How does your relationship with where you grew up affect the way you view the world? Does it color your experiences and worldviews even into adulthood?

The Chippewa's Dream Catchers, while misunderstood and appropriated outside of Native communities, are of high significance in the larger culture, especially when you take into account how seriously the community takes their dreams and vision quests. Having a well-rounded comprehension of just how important this spiritual item is makes it much easier to understand why it's so meaningful to the Chippewa, specifically.

The Sioux's reverence for familial bonds runs so deep that they created the Hunka Ceremony to unite unrelated people. It speaks to how strongly they view the need for connection and brotherhood and is a lovely example of how they embrace people and treat them as their own. Deepening ties to your loved ones, friends, and your own community doesn't require a formal Ceremony. It can be as simple as helping a neighbor with their weeding or giving an elderly relative a phone call.

The Chumash have been nearly wiped off the record. History is still not doing right by them. But this beautiful, peace-filled Nation has produced magical, magnetic, and enthralling cave art and handcrafts. Their gentle and harmonious relationship to the environment made the world where they lived abundant for them. Their enduring legacy and contributions are deserving of attention and will serve to make the world a more balanced place.

Let what you have learned about Native American spirituality and culture inform the way you treat those around you and how you move through the world. Once we know more about how other cultures move through the world, we can do better in our own circles. And now that you've learned how interconnected Native American spiritual worldviews are, you can see the ways in which all the greater aspects of your own life are interlinked. Do you have a spiritual practice that informs how you treat others? Can your values be reflected in how you regard the environment at large? How can you further fundamental ideals (like that of the Seventh Generation), being in harmony with nature, and appreciating the gifts you've been given without co-opting Native American Traditions?

CONCLUSION

All of the Native American Nations discussed in this book are active and thriving to this day. Despite everything they've endured, they do the work of keeping their culture and beliefs alive for the benefit of the younger generations and to honor the people who came before them and suffered deeply—all the while trying to stand up for their own humanity and right to exist. The mere act of educating ourselves about Native culture can make non-Natives better equipped to walk through the world with a lighter touch.

Moving forward, you now have the foundational tools to continue your education. Each of these Nations has robust information both online at their official websites and at their physical community centers. The best way to learn more is to go straight to the source. Find ways to support the Native American Nation in your community. Anyone living in North America is living on stolen Native lands. Find out who your local Tribe is. Learn about their history, both the good and the bad. Check out online and physical resources that will give you a more thorough understanding about their particular experience.

Compare and contrast what you previously thought you already knew about your local Native American Nation and their experiences, past and present, with the information you can access now. Are there any glaring omissions or egregious errors? Have you found discrepancies between what you thought you knew and what the reality is?

By getting an honest education about the land where you were born, you pave the way for meaningful allyship. There will never be a better or more appropriate teacher than Native Americans themselves. Getting involved with your local community is the most authentic way you can learn more, forge connections, and embody these values in an appropriate way. Don't be afraid to ask hard questions of yourself and others and examine why you may have had certain misconceptions and preconceived notions.

A willingness to self-interrogate, even when there are hard truths to uncover, is a surefire way to grow. The moment non-Natives are able to humble themselves—realizing that their knowledge has been limited as a result of centuries of colonization and oppression—the doors to true understanding and brotherhood are thrown wide open.

RESOURCES

If you are interested in learning more about Native American Nations, visit their websites, connect with their Leaders, and become involved with your local Tribe.

The Cherokee Nation
https://www.cherokee.org

The Chinook Nation
https://chinooknation.org

Delaware Lenape Tribal Nation
https://delawaretribe.org

The Haudenosaunee Confederacy
https://www.haudenosauneeconfederacy.com/who-we-are

Lenape Nation of Pennsylvania
https://www.lenape-nation.org

Nanticoke Lenni-Lenape Tribal Nation
https://nlltribe.com/about-us

The Navajo Nation
https://www.navajo-nsn.gov

THE CHIPPEWA NATION

Minnesota Chippewa Tribe
https://www.mnchippewatribe.org

Saginaw Chippewa Tribe
http://www.sagchip.org

Sault Tribe
https://www.saulttribe.com

THE SIOUX NATION

Cheyenne River Sioux Tribe
https://www.cheyenneriversiouxtribe.org

Coastal Band of the Chumash Nation
https://coastalbandofthechumashnation.weebly.com

Great Lakota, Nakota, Dakota Nation
https://lakotadakotanakotanation.org

The Northern Chumash Tribe
https://northernchumash.org

Rosebud Sioux Tribe
https://www.rosebudsiouxtribe-nsn.gov

Santa Ynez Chumash Nation
https://www.santaynezchumash.org

Standing Rock Sioux Tribe
https://standingrock.org

The Water Protector movement began in 2016 with the Standing Rock Sioux Tribe. Driven by the respect for water taught by sacred practices, Water Protectors continue to defend waterways across North America to this day.

ABOUT THE AUTHOR

L. M. Arroyo is a writer, journalist, and author residing in New York City. This writer sees herself only as a conduit of the material itself. The true authors of this book are the Elders and other Native American individuals who are the source of each Nation's Traditional Knowledge and Oral Traditions. No one outside of these Native American Nations can claim authorship over any of this information. Given the centuries of persecution that Native Americans have endured, the survival of this information is a testament to the determined resilience of the keepers of this Sacred Knowledge. They are the ones responsible for keeping their Traditions, spirituality, beliefs, and practices alive and flourishing, to the benefit of their People and to the non-Native population who long to learn more.

INDEX

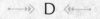

D

G

First published in 2023 by Wellfleet Press, an imprint of The Quarto Group,
142 West 36th Street, 4th Floor, New York, NY 10018, USA
T (212) 779-4972 F (212) 779-6058 www.Quarto.com

Wellfleet titles are also available at discount for retail, wholesale, promotional, and bulk
purchase. For details, contact the Special Sales Manager by email at specialsales@quarto.com
or by mail at The Quarto Group, Attn: Special Sales Manager, 100 Cummings Center Suite
265D, Beverly, MA 01915 USA.

10 9 8 7 6 5 4 3 2 1

ISBN: 978-1-57715-358-0

Library of Congress Control Number: 2023931197

Publisher: Rage Kindelsperger
Creative Director: Laura Drew
Managing Editor: Cara Donaldson
Editor: Sara Bonacum
Cover and Interior Design: Amelia LeBarron

Printed in China

This book provides general information on various widely known and widely accepted images
that tend to evoke feelings of strength and confidence. However, it should not be relied upon
as recommending or promoting any specific diagnosis or method of treatment for a particular
condition, and it is not intended as a substitute for medical advice or for direct diagnosis
and treatment of a medical condition by a qualified physician. Readers who have questions
about a particular condition, possible treatments for that condition, or possible reactions
from the condition or its treatment should consult a physician or other qualified healthcare
professional.